Shades and Curves of my Life

Life Never Gives Up On Those Who Never Give Up On Life

Sudeep Verma

INDIA • SINGAPORE • MALAYSIA

Notion Press Media Pvt Ltd

No. 50, Chettiyar Agaram Main Road,
Vanagaram, Chennai, Tamil Nadu – 600 095

First Published by Notion Press 2022

ISBN 979-8-88521-482-7

Dedicated to:

Ma & Pa

Mentor – Pradeep Kumar,

Believer – Moti Chand Gaur,

Soul Mate – Vivek Verma

Lifeline – Annie and Vatsal

To those who Dream and Embark on the journey of life

To those who TEACH, GIVE and BELIEVE.

The journey of life has many curves, taking us up and down on its path revealing various shades of life. Life is the best teacher and the real-life experiences, the best source for learning. Change is the constant that keeps life's heartbeat ticking. Continuous learning often changes the course of our intended path.

The curves of the author's life, a common, average guy next door, have taken him through extreme ups and downs, surprise turns and twists, love and heartbreak, unexpected bumps and shocks, knowledge trees and the flowers of learning, the desert of dejection and mountains of happiness. Sailing through these curves of life has enriched him with wisdom that comes only through real-life experiences.

This book narrates some of the true incidents that unfolded during thirteen years on the curves of his life and left him with many valuable and positive lessons. The narration shares the spirit of the incident and not the exact words used. The motive behind writing this book is to leave the reader with a positive outlook on life. It is to reassure the reader that despite hurdles and challenges one can go on the path of success, happiness by adopting a path of passion, perseverance, patience, and positivity with the help of a mentor. The narrative in the book does not criticize anybody, rather it's for self-reflection & self-improvement.

Acknowledgment

My mother, who is the biggest reason for who I am today. She is my best friend, believer, love of my life, guru, and a true support system. My father, who impressed me with his pure heart and selflessness. He injected traits of a traveler, writer, honesty, and dedication in me.

My wife, who is the backbone of my life. Without her support, I could not have sailed through my life. My son, who is the love of my life and the biggest motivation in my quest for life. My family, Madhurima, Gopal Ji, Garima, Dr. Sanjay, Dhirendra, and Manju for their love and support. Prakhar-Nidhi, Aastha-Ruchit, Saakshi-Sunny, and Tejas, Srijan are the closest to my heart and the sources of energy.

My uncle, Moti Chand Gaur, motivated and believed in me during my worst time, instilling much-needed hope and confidence.

My mentor and guru, Pradeep Kumar aka PK, made me a professional. His advice, guidance and motivation changed my life for good.

My soulmate, Vivek Verma, with whom I believe to have a connection from many past-lives. He gave me the best and most practical pieces of advice which have helped me at the critical juncture of my life.

My dearest friends who believed in me unconditionally and stood by me whenever, I needed them. They hold a special place in my heart.

PK, Annie, Dipti, for their invaluable inputs to complete my first book.

Prologue

I was lying on a bed in the waiting area of the operation ward outside the operation theater of the Oncology ward of the Max Hospital, Vaishali. I was diagnosed with Colon Cancer, and the reports showed that it has reached some nodes outside the colon area and may be spreading in the body. Dr. Harit Chaturvedi, Chairman – Max Institute of Cancer Care, in Max hospital had diagnosed the colon cancer and was about to operate. I bid farewell to my wife one last time, not knowing if we would see each other again. Though, I had been hopeful that everything would be fine. My thought process has changed over the years. I have a strong belief that the soul never dies but, the body does. I also believe that souls meet again and again in different lives before they reach nirvana (out of lifecycle). This thought helped me think that either, I will be operated successfully and will meet all my loved ones in this life once again or, this may be the end of this life for me and I will go back to 'the ultimate home' now and may not be able to see my loved ones again in this life.

I was lying in a relaxed mode. I saw a whiteboard on the wall where my name was fourth in sequence and, there were tick marks against the first two names. There was no mark against the third person, who went just before me. I assumed that this person must be getting operated inside the operation theater. I took a deep breath and tried to meditate. I get into meditation mode quite effortlessly. But this time, I could not as there was a little bit of anxiety. I must mention that this indeed was the anxiety and not the worry. It was the anxiety of getting over with the operation.

A team of three doctors came to me and asked, "how are you doing?"

"I am doing fine and waiting for my turn," I smiled.

"That is very heartening to hear that you feel fine," he responded.

"I know that you guys are the best and will do what is best possible. I am giving my body to you guys just do what you need to do," I said.

"A positive attitude is the best healer and, it helps us as well," he said.

"All the very best to you guys," I laughed in a low tone.

"I want to tell you about the process. We will give you epidural anesthesia in the back...," he started explaining the process.

"Yes, I am aware of that. My sister, Dr. Kirti Saxena, and niece, Dr. Aastha Srivastava Khera, are Anesthetists and, I have been advised about it," I interrupted humbly.

He was amazed at my awareness and explained a few other things.

"When is my turn to be operated?" I asked curiously.

"Unfortunately, we are running late with earlier critical surgeries so it may take at least 30-45 minutes more," the senior Doctor responded.

"Oh God! I wanted to get over with this as quickly as possible. Ok, I will wait but, please inform my wife outside about this delay else, she will be worried thinking why it is taking longer for the surgery," I requested.

"Sure, will do that," he said and, they left.

I tried to meditate again so that the time pass, quickly. But despite my trying harder, I could not meditate due to my restlessness. Then I started analyzing my life and, the whole life flashed back. I looked back and realized that my life had taken me through many turns-twists, ups-downs, moments of dejections and ecstasy, love and heartbreak, and has given me many invaluable lessons. I thought, "an interesting movie, can be made out of this." I remembered my father sharing his life learning which impacted me positively. "If the operation is successful, I will write a book on these learnings and share with the world. So much has happened in my life that I can write at least a few books," I thought.

Time has passed since and, this is the first book I am writing reflecting back at thirteen crucial years of my life.

Chapter 1

The year 1988

Nainital – my favorite hill station. I had always found some kind of umbilical cord connection with this majestic place. I had always loved this place due to its overall beauty consisting of beautiful Naini lake surrounded by lush-green gorgeous mountains, wonderful weather throughout the year, and of course amazing native people.

I loved hiking in the morning and that day, I was trekking to the China Peak, the highest peak of this lovely city. I was feeling very happy inside and started my brisk walk uphill. Due to my enthusiasm and target to reach the peak early, I took a shortcut through a mountain nallah which usually is dry except during rainy seasons. I was young, thin, and very agile so, I quickly climbed to the top after taking a few quick shortcuts. I reached the top of China-Peak and was breathing heavily. I was feeling very happy to reach there quickly. I was eager to see the majestic view of the Nainital city with the beautiful Naini lake which looks like the shape of a shell.

Confident, I reached the viewpoint and loved the mesmerizing view of Nainital lake and the city from the top. I felt like embracing this heart-touching view. I went near the edge, closed my eyes, spread my arms, and shouted "Nainital, I love youuuu." In that state, I took one step ahead without realizing much, and suddenly, I slipped. I desperately tried to hold onto anything but that part of the land was rocky with small gravels on it which caused the slip. I could not get hold of anything and fell from the cliff. I felt the butterflies in my stomach due to the fall. I could see death in front of me and I felt the sweat in my body. Any moment I could steal from gravity, I prayed, "please God, save me, I don't want to die."

I saw the rock beneath and tried to close my eyes. And then I hit the ground below. Oh, God.

I felt the pain, and my eyes opened. Oh, thank God I am alive. I had fallen from the bed and realized it was a dream where I felt the gravity due to falling from my bed. I finally could smile after the dream of a virtual death experience. I saw the morning sunlight peeping into the bedroom through the window.

I could see various small particles dancing in the sunlight. This is the Brownian motion as taught in Physics. They are light particles of dust roaming in the air. I realized that falling from bed in fact gave me that feeling of weightlessness and the butterfly in the stomach like we get while going down in a giant wheel. I laughed, "thank you Mr. Newton, and your laws."

My father was posted in Nainital for a year when I was in class 5. With Nainital, it was a love at first sight. I instantly felt a connection with that mesmerizing city. Even after my father's transfer to Lucknow, I used to travel to Nainital frequently due to that heavenly connection. Despite the virtual deathly fall in my dream, I still felt happy seeing that mesmerizing city view.

PHYSICS was my LIFE. I used to visualize physics everywhere. I was doing my Masters in Physics from the prestigious Lucknow University. The love affair with physics had started only a few years back when I learned that to know more about the outer space, I need to join ISRO or BARC, and gaining an expertise in Physics could help get there. I was doing something which I loved and hence the love affair.

We were living in Kaisarbagh officer's colony, a central place in Lucknow, close to happening city places like Ameenabad, Kaisarbagh, and Hazratganj; all of them at a walking distance of

5-10 minutes. Lucknow University was also hardly 10 minutes walk across river Gomti and via my favorite Hanuman Setu temple. Kaisarbagh officers' colony was a newly constructed four-story apartment complex with a total of 64 flats in the colony. It used to be called Kaisarbagh officers' colony as it was built for the state, central government officers besides judges, Doctors, journalists, and other distinguished persons. The atmosphere of the colony was fantastic with a lot of like-minded and the right age group people living there. There was new energy and positivity in the atmosphere. This was the best time of my life.

M.Sc. first-year final exams were only a few days away. I had worked very hard through the year and was feeling confident but at the same time was anxious to get done with it quickly.

The time of the exams came. The first exam was a practical test and I went to the lab with a positive attitude. The beginning of the final exam was good as my practical went pretty well, the lab work as well as the viva. I started preparing for the written exams with all my positive energy. The first two papers on 'Methods of Mathematical Physics' and 'Classical and Statistical Mechanics' went pretty well. The next paper was 'Electromagnetic, Electrodynamics & Electronics', I looked at the paper and found myself good on four questions, while on one question, I was not very strong but was ok about it. I started writing the paper and planned to complete the four questions, where I was strong, first, to score more. Due to my slow writing speed and deep involvement, I realized that the first three questions had taken 80% of my exam time. I started rushing and answered the fourth question crisply and shortly. Now, I had only 10 minutes left for the fifth question. I still tried to move fast and answered what best I could have but of course, it left me unsatisfied. After the exam, I reflected and understood the need and urgency of the remaining papers to go extremely well. I pulled up my socks and got into 24X7 mode of urgency and started revising the chapters.

The fourth paper was on 'Introductory Quantum Mechanics, Atomic & Molecular Spectra.' This was my area of strength, so, I was confident as well as determined to cover the lost ground in the previous paper. I was sitting in the first row in the exam hall just opposite the examiner's desk. I looked at the paper and felt delighted as the paper was of my choice and I was very comfortable with questions. I started answering the first question and got deeply involved in writing with speed. This time, I did not want to loose time and get in a situation like the last paper, where due to lack of time I could not complete two questions satisfactorily. I had completed answering around 80% of the first question when, I heard some commotion in the room and outside the room. I decided not to waste time so did not look around to see what was happening. Suddenly, one scrambled paper in the form of a crunched ball landed in front of me on my desk. My concentration broke and I looked at the paper and took it in my hand trying to understand what it was. I looked back in the examination room to understand who threw it and I could not see any head raised. I turned back to report it to the examiner but instead found a flying squad examiner standing in front of me.

A flying squad is a set of external examiners who make surprise visits to various exam centers to prevent cheating.

I realized the commotion was of a flying squad coming in and that is why there were sounds of unrest inside the examination hall. Before, I could say anything, the flying squad examiner took hold of paper from my hand and shouted at me, "You are cheating..........?"

I WAS PERPLEXED, SHOCKED, AND FURIOUS WITH THE QUESTION.

Chapter 2

Lying on the rooftop of our house when I was a kid, I used to see millions of stars in the sky. My curiosity had led me to ask many questions about the stars and galaxy to whomsoever, I could have asked. I learned about the galaxy, our solar system, and that there are many more solar systems. And then came the fun-part, trying to locate the constellations in the sky. My favorite was 'Saptrishi Ashram' and some other constellations besides 'Dhruv Tara' the North Star. I used to watch these stars for hours especially in summers when often we used to sleep on the rooftop. I wondered what must be on these stars, what is their constitution and would there be life elsewhere in any of the planets in these galaxies?

This curiosity further got complex when, I used to see people talking about astrology and how these star movements can predict what lies ahead in one's life. On top of that, I also learned that Palmistry also has linkages with stars and can predict the future. That added another dimension to my inquisitiveness. When, I grew-up a little more, besides looking at the galaxy and stars, I started reading books on astrology and Palmistry like Cheiro, Narayan Dutt Srimali, Linda Goodman, and others. Though, I never went too deep, yet I started seeing astrology charts and started looking at other people's hands after reading palmistry. This grew my interest further. I gained significant knowledge and was happy to see that I was getting attention among family and friends. This further motivated me.

As I grew older and came into higher classes, the *Star Treck* series started getting telecasted on TV, and that became my favorite TV serial, as it used to show exactly what I loved – space voyages, exploring stars, new curious adventures, and possible life on new planets. I still remember the theme of the

Star Treck series "*Space, the final frontier. These are the voyages of the starship enterprise, it's a five-year mission to explore strange new worlds, to seek out new life, new civilizations, to boldly go where no man had gone before.*" I used to be hooked to the adventures of *Captain James T Kirk,* but my favorite character in the series was *Mr. Spock* with his no-nonsense attitude and knowledge of the starship. This serial had further added fuel to my interest in the outer world – THE SPACE.

Around my college days, my interest grew in the space race between the United States of America and the Soviet Union (which later got divided into 15 countries including Russia). I used to keenly watch the news related to space excursions of these two superpowers. Initially, I was confused as to why Americans mentioned their space-traveling team as Astronauts and why Soviets used to call them Cosmonauts. In the early days of space exploration and the politics at play during that time, it was important for America and Russia to differentiate the people being trained to go on missions in space. After all, they were in a very serious competition with each other and it's not surprising that they've chosen different names despite this being the same role, essentially. Like many of the words used in the scientific world, the name attributed to the brave people sent to space takes its root in ancient Greek.

The word Astronaut is made of the prefix "Astro" which means stars and the suffix "naut" which means sailor. An astronaut is essentially ***a star sailor***.

1. The word Cosmonaut is made of the prefix "Cosmo" which means universe and the same suffix as above is "naut". And so, a cosmonaut is a ***sailor of the universe***.

2. Semantically speaking, the difference between them is not that big.

My first exciting moment in this direction came when my father was posted in Nainital, as the joint director of Tourism for the Uttar Pradesh government (in an undivided Uttar Pradesh). I came to know that Nainital has an observatory called ARIES. Aryabhatta Research Institute of Observational Sciences (ARIES) is a leading research institute in Nainital, Uttarakhand. The institute specializes in Astronomy, Solar Physics, Astrophysics, and Atmospheric sciences.

This was a fantastic news for my curiosity and hunger for outer space knowledge, and I immediately convinced my father to take me to the observatory to have a closer look at the stars from the large telescopes installed there. My magical moment arrived and I went inside the observatory. I got to see the Moon with a very close look. I saw the deep craters in golden color (unlike the silver color moon visible through naked eyes). Then I saw Jupiter, which was quite big but still smaller than the golden moon that we see. And then I saw Saturn visible with its rings. I was ecstatic, a feeling of fulfillment came to me, yet at the same time, my hunger and curiosity to watch and learn more about the divinely SPACE, the final frontier, grew stronger.

As per my family, relatives, and friends, I was a very soft-spoken, and a shy type of person. My focus in studies was due to the influence of my elder sisters, Madhurima and Garima, who were very good students. My younger sister, Garima, specifically was a big influence on me as she always topped her classes and was a favorite of her teachers. In my home, my parents were from the arts side and not the science side. My mother did her graduation from Banaras Hindu University (BHU), Varanasi in the 1950s, which was a very remarkable thing in her time. My father did his graduation from the Allahabad University in History as a major and was deeply in love with History. His knowledge of history was outstanding. Both my elder sisters too opted for their higher studies in the art side. My brother, Dhirendra, had opted for his higher studies in the Commerce side. When it came to the science side there was no guidance for me from my family. I was interested in science, so, I typically had two options, opt for the mathematics side towards the engineering line or opt for biology towards the medical line. Since, I did not like cutting a frog, I did not opt for biology, and instead, I opted for PCM (physics, chemistry, and mathematics) in my high school and intermediate thinking of opting for an engineering career for myself. I started preparing for engineering as everyone else was doing. In the mid-80s there were only seven government engineering colleges and no private engineering college in Uttar Pradesh. There was only one very tough and competitive combined engineering exam (called MNR) to get into these seven engineering colleges. But during intermediate exams and after that I went through a serious health issue and as a result, I could not give my best and did not qualify for engineering. Though, I and everyone at home knew that I could not give my best due to bad health conditions, yet it indeed was seen as a debacle and left a big impact on me as most of my friends had got admission to engineering colleges. Reactions of surprise came from family, friends, relatives, and neighbors which impacted me tremendously. This was the biggest shock of my life.

I started analyzing what went wrong with me and out of a few root causes, two problems primarily stood out, my bad health condition and my speed of writing the answers. However, in this case, bad health played a major role and caused big disappointment. My mother told me that this is your bad luck and not the lack of knowledge. All mothers support their children. She insisted to take me to an astrologer. Though, I was interested in astrology, yet I had never visited any astrologer. I believed that knowing about the future will not help because if something wrong is predicted then the worry of that will negatively impact the present, and if something good is predicted then the prior knowledge of that will take away the excitement and joy of the actual happy moment. However, when one goes through bad times, the curiosity to know the future increases.

I visited the astrologer. The astrologer looked at my chart carefully and started mumbling, as if talking to himself and then he said that my stars are such that they will always impact my studies and outcome. He specifically said something about my bad Mercury. He gave some remedies which my mother noted but my mind was wandering not on what he said about me but on the science of astrology.

I came back and discussed the same with my uncle, Moti Chand Gaur, who did his engineering from Roorkee Engineering College in the 1960s and was an executive engineer in PWD. He also had a great interest in astrology and possessed a deep knowledge of reading charts. He heard me and looked at my charts and told me two things:

"As per your birth lagan charts, you are destined to reach great heights of success, much more than anyone can believe." I heard him and actually could not believe him given my current situation.

"Though as per my understanding of your chart, you will get involved in business and leadership. But my general **advice** to you is that you must pursue your dreams and if you like stars, space then institutions like ISRO (Indian Space Research Organization) or BARC (Bhabha Atomic Research Centre) are the gateways. And to get into these institutions, your physics and mathematics must be very strong which we know is the case anyways. You should pursue higher studies in Physics," he said. And it felt like a light bulb of realization switched-on in my head. PHYSICS, yes, of course, it makes perfect sense as I liked physics so far anyways.

THE ADVICE made perfect sense to me. I got a new direction, and for the first-time it was an advice, which was well thought of and of my interest. A career in the area of my interest will be a dream come true. I got my real mission. The destination is ISRO or BARC and the companion is PHYSICS. And that's how, I began my Love Affair with Physics. I got admission in graduation with PCM subjects and completed my graduation successfully.

At this age of my life, there were so many friends around me who were engaged in love affairs. The concept of 'forced vibration' in physics (**Forced vibrations** occur if something is continuously driven by an external force) was also playing its role in my real life. While, I was having my affair with physics, my friends and cousins around me were involved in love affairs. This sort of invoked a feeling in me as well, though, I was trying to suppress the same. One of my known persons, Kalpana, and I were attracted towards each other and while I was trying to suppress my feelings yet, I knew I was falling for her too. And before I could do anything to stop it, we both finally fell for each other. Now, I had two loves in life– Physics, and Kalpana. Life indeed was beautiful. Since, I really wanted to focus on my dream career, I was conscious that I have to strike the balance. Age-wise, I was more mature so, I discussed with her that love cannot impact our studies. Though we agreed, yet it was difficult for her to understand at times as she was much younger than me. Often, I used to force both of us to focus on studies, despite this being not easy for me either.

I kept my focus intact on doing M.Sc. in physics and appeared in the much-awaited entrance exams for Masters in Physics in the prestigious Lucknow University (yes, at that time there used to be a tough competitive entrance exam to get admission in M.Sc. Physics in Lucknow University.) I got selected in the entrance exam and took my affair with physics to the next level of commitment. I worked hard in the first year and prepared well. And now, it was time for me to appear in the first-year final exams of M.Sc. Physics.

Coming back to the incident:

"I am not a cheater; someone has just thrown this paper on my table," I lost control and blurted. I was very angry since this was the first time anyone was accusing me wrongly and that too for cheating which, I never believed in and which was against my value system.

"Every cheater says this only," the flying squad invigilator got further angry at my tone and spoke.

"What is this nonsense," I thought.

"I don't know what is in this paper and if you can find anything matching in my answer sheet then I will do whatever you will say," I was losing my precious exam time so somehow, I tried to control my anger and told him. I was pretty sure that nothing will match as this was not my paper anyways.

"Shut-up! *Chori aur seenajori*," instead of understanding my point, invigilator's ego got hurt and he got further aggravated and shouted.

This was too much for my values and self-respect besides, I was losing much precious time to complete my paper. I was exasperated.

"The hell with you. I am not a cheater and have NEVER cheated. *Jao exam nahi dena* (I won't give exam)," I shouted at him and threw my answer sheet at his face. This was too big an attack on my value system, so, instead of a calm response, I reacted at him violently, in frustration and anger.

And without much normal thinking, I walked out of the exam hall in anger and huff with my face burning like fire.

And that was it. I picked up my bicycle from the university stand and came back home with all drastic emotions in my mind and with a feeling of numbness. **My DREAM was just SHATTERED** into million pieces and on top of that, I was accused falsely against my honest VALUE & BELIEF system which I just can't compromise. Someone's mischievous act shattered my dreams and it felt just like a terrorist attack killing an innocent life.

"You came back so early?" Mom was surprised to see me back.

I did not say anything controlling my broken heart in a state of impassiveness. Mothers know well if something goes wrong with their kids and she also sensed that something unusual had happened.

"How did the paper go?" she again asked.

"I left the paper mid-way ...," I said, in a very low and cracked voice, trying to control my emotions and heartbreak.

She was shocked as she had seen my undivided passion, focus, solid preparations, and confidence, and hence she could not understand why I left the paper in between. I was sitting on my chair in my room with my head hung low and body in a give-up posture.

"What happened, son?" She stroked my head and asked lovingly.

And with that touch of my mother, who is the closest person in my life, I just broke down in tears, uncontrollably. Without using my mouth, I was sharing my inner thoughts through my tears, that now everything has gone – dream shattered; self-respect has been stabbed; PHYSICS, my life, has evaded, divorcing me, and ISRO/BARC has eluded me and escaped out of reach. She hugged me, taking me in her arms. I had always found comfort, solace, and love in my mother's arms but this time, I was completely blank, numb, and lost.

"Somebody threw a jumbled paper on my desk and I have been falsely accused of cheating. I just could not bear the false accusation and left the paper in between," I explained to her in short.

"How anybody can throw their paper on your table? How can the invigilator accuse you without understanding the actual incident? Being elder and mature, they should have heard and at least looked into what was written in that paper and try to match in the answer sheet," she was perplexed and angry too while trying to console me.

I was still blank and disoriented, and not listening. She put my head in her lap and continued stroking my head. I don't know when I slept but I woke after hours of sleep. My mother was with me all along this time. Once I got up, she again tried to console me repeating her prior words as to how such a thing can happen. This time, I was listening with relative calmness. And this is the first time it hit me hard as to what have I done and what has happened. Leaving paper in between means the end of the road for me, my dreams are actually shattered. My life was Physics, ISRO/BARC and now that is not the case anymore.

"How much of the paper you had attempted before leaving?" my mother logically asked me.

"Paper was pretty good; I knew all the answers. I was about to finish the first question before all that happened and I left," I spoke.

"You can still give the final paper as your first three papers had gone fine. You will get low marks in the fourth paper but on average with all five papers you can still sail through the first year," she understood the gravity but still suggested me.

The first thought that came to mind was that leaving one paper in between means they may fail me and even if I pass it, I will not be able to get much-needed marks which, I was told, was the main criteria for ISRO/BARC. But most importantly, with such false humiliation, how will I face my teachers and classmates as I had left in between. Though I know, I am innocent, others may not believe it. Though my image was very clean yet it was my inner perception of "Log kya kahenge (what will people say)", a typical syndrome of our Indian society. So, I refused to go back and join. Mother kept on impressing me to rejoin but I guess, my value system and self-respect were so much hurt that I could not understand any other argument at that time and were firm on my stand of dropping M.Sc. Physics.

The only thought going on in my mind was:

"IS THIS THE END OF MY LIFE?"

Chapter 3

The Curves of Steep Downfall

The news of my dropping my M.Sc. in Physics spread pretty fast among my family, relatives, friends, and neighborhood. And everywhere the initial reaction was that this cannot be true so people started trying to connect with me and my family to know more about what exactly happened. While my mindset was very low yet people still asked the question. I tried to avoid and a sense of dejection set in me. A few classmates from M.Sc. came and they also tried to convince me to join back but by this time my self-confidence had gone in a free-fall mode (a different type of gravity force taking me into a black hole), so I did not change my decision. My point remained that what about my self-respect and secondly, with loss of marks ISRO/BARC seems impossible.

My father also tried to convince me, rather in a pushy manner, to join back M.Sc. but I was relentless. He became really upset with me and asked "What will you do now?" to which I had no answer. I knew all parents love their kids. While mothers are more emotionally attached and are expressive, fathers are generally a little tough at times to push their points. It has been said "Father's daughters and Mother's son" which means fathers are softer towards their daughters than sons and on the other hand mothers are softer towards sons. The same was the case in our house as well. My father, who I knew for a fact loves me, was a little harsh with me at the time since he felt, I was being stubborn and not accepting the practical solution (in his opinion.) One day a friend of his came home and asked about me. My father told him, "*Nalayak hai* (He is stupid), does not listens to me. He has dropped his masters in physics and he has no clue what to do next." These words pierced through my heart as my state of mind was in a bad shape. I felt like a 'Rebel', though afterward, thinking with a calm mind, I understood that he cares for me and was only concerned.

I could easily see the change in the attitude of many people who once loved me and respected me. They now started either ignoring me or started criticizing me. It was very difficult to go out of home and my social circle reduced tremendously which put me in a shell. I remained locked in my room as much as possible.

Till the M.Sc. debacle, everyone expected me to do well in my career so, everyone treated me with love and respect. But now the same people started doubting me, and some who knew about it even started commenting on my distraction due to my affair with Kalpana. I knew this was not the case. There may have been a 5%-10% impact on my studies, but I worked harder to cover it.

Till now, my affair with Kalpana was known only to my mother in my family besides some close friends, but it was not known to her parents. And my image was very good in their mind. They saw me as a very sincere, focused, and a good boy who is determined to achieve big success. They used to ask Kalpana to take tips from me on some subjects, especially mathematics. These interactions and her liking of me slowly converted into mutual liking which ultimately converted into a love affair over a while. Now, with me slipping into depression Kalpana got concerned and used to try to reach me while, I used to be locked in my room. One day Kalpana's mother found out about our affair. Her mother was shocked and felt betrayed, rightly so. But, I had not planned this affair, it just happened despite my trying very hard not to fall for it. This was another shock for me and added to my misery as it was a direct attack on my self-respect and value system. I wished that she would have known that how hard we restricted ourselves and instead we kept our focus on our studies. Many of my friends indulged in physical intimation with their girlfriends/boyfriends but we restrained ourselves.

Sometimes, I feel that there should be a recorder with Almighty God that can be replayed in such situations. Like the flying-squad, invigilator could have seen that I was not a cheater; Kalpana's mother could have seen that I had not betrayed her and rather how much, I protected her daughter; How much, I protected her from few 'adventurous' minded people around. But then this never happens. As they say in astrology when the stars are bad everything goes wrong. This was like the last nail in the coffin. I felt, I hit rock bottom in my life.

Locked in my room, I started thinking. How come a few disappointments in studies or competitive exams can change the attitude of people towards me while I am the same person with the same heart, personality, attitude, and traits. To an extent, I understood that people look at outcomes to recognize a person but what I still could not understand was why they cannot recognize my pure heart, behavior, attitude, and intent which has not changed at all. This changed attitude of society further aggravated the rebel inside me. I became very angry, very furious– like a Rebel. At the same time, I was completely dejected and clueless regarding my future course of action. At times, a feeling to end my life did occur to me but good sense prevailed and I realized that this is not right.

I started visiting Hanuman-Setu temple, my favorite place for a long time. From my childhood, I have seen my mother devoting herself to God besides doing her Karma. Thanks to her teachings, I also believed in Karma and Worship. But now, I was very angry with Hanuman Ji as well. I started visiting the temple quite often. Looking straight into the eyes of Hanuman Ji, I asked him "Why this is happening to me?

You know very well that I did nothing wrong, either in exams or with Kalpana, so why am I facing all this misery?" The calm smile on his face used to calm down my anger a bit after a while and I used to find some solace. I used to sit there for hours and try to calm myself. I also had been taught by my mother that life, of most people, goes through ups and downs throughout and that perseverance with patience and positivity is the mantra for a successful life. Looking around, I did find this logic right. The life of most people does not remain the same forever, it does go through the curves of good and bad times many times. I prayed to Hanuman Ji, that since I am already at rock bottom of my life, please bring on the rest of the bad times, that may have been planned in my life, at this time and till the age of 25 years itself, after which, 'IF' I survive then I should have a good stable life.

I was clueless, with constant questions in my mind – "What next, which direction to go and what are my options now?" While 'The Rebel' in me was furious like a hulk yet the 'Clueless Person' in me with shattered confidence was unaware of which direction to go.

THE ADVICE:

I discussed this with my best friend, Vivek Verma.

"Why people cannot accept me in the same manner in which they used to, before this debacle. What success has to do with the acceptability of a good human being?" I asked.

"Society looks at both, a materialistically successful person as well as a good human being. Only a good human being is not sufficient for society in general. If you are not materialistically successful then you will not get good recognition or acceptance, instead, you may be pitied or criticized," he responded with clarity.

"You have three choices. First, do not live with this society and take your good heart and go for renunciation: Second, live within the society and do not care about what they have to say; Third, live within the society and be successful materialistically with Position and Money," he continued. "It is not as bad to be materialistically successful irrespective of what people think, as this is a more practical way to be recognized and live in a society. So, the third option is not that bad. With your focus, hard work, and orientation you can turn the tables around if you want to," he suggested the option and gave me confidence. I was angry and devastated and this advice was a hard-hitting truth. But this was practical. Society does recognize and respects a materialistically successful person. Being good at heart is not enough.

Choice:

For me, becoming a person with a good heart was more important than being materialistically successful. But being a people's person, I cannot live without family, relatives, friends even though I was deeply hurt by many of them. I also knew that if I am not successful then I will be rejected by Kalpana's parents. This thought left me with the only choice of making a comeback. This was not only a choice but a retaliation to shut the fuck this society. I did not know my career options, but I was sure that I will turn the tables around and I will become a damn successful person. Though it is not typically my personality, yet I chose "Retaliation" as my way forward to respond to society.

My decision: Falling is not an option. I deliberated way forward options:

- Option-1: Target Information Technology and Computer Science line, as a career, as per the advice, to quickly gain the lost ground. With the rise of computerization, automation, and growth in that line, the sky is the limit as I found out.

- Option-2: Try for Public Services Commission exams which will boost my image. However, this was a tough and long approach with some risks embedded in it due to my lost time.

I thought, I will dig deeper on both options and may try for both.

I resolved to become materialistically successful for sure.

Chapter 4

I started my deep research to understand my options.

In the late 1980s, there was a huge surge in Computer Science and Computer Application jobs primarily led by the huge demand from the USA and some European countries. The USA and Europe had already seen the quality of the talent force coming from India in the areas of Medical Sciences as well as Engineering and specifically in the space of Computer Science in the 1960s and 1970s. This was because the leading Indian educational institutions, like IITs and IIMs, produced the best of the talents, and since there were limited opportunities within India, these resources used to be highly sought after in the western world which was going through tremendous advancement in these areas. And since the cost of these resources was relatively cheaper compared to hiring a local native due to the difference in the currency rate, Indians were more sought after. By the 1970s, the quality of the Indian talent force was very well established in the western worlds of the USA and Europe. Companies, saw huge benefits in terms of intellect and cost, and as a result, they started hiring more and more talent force from India. This was a major loss to India as its best talents were hijacked by these international companies. However, these Indians who used to become NRIs (Non-Resident Indians) used to earn in western countries and send back some money to their families back in India which gave a boost to the Indian economy as well. By the mid-1980s, this demand grew significantly as the companies wanted to be more competitive and profitable. Parallelly, in India, economic liberalization started. This further gave a boost to many sectors but specifically to the Information Technology sector. Many Indian companies started investing heavily in the information technology sector. As there was a huge surge in the need for computerization and automation by the International as well as Indian companies, there was a huge surge in demand for Indian resources in the information technology sector. By the late 1980s, the demand grew quite high, with projections of further growth.

With my focus on Physics and the target of ISRO, I was ignorant of this development in the country and the world, and rightly so, because I was following my passion, and money and materialistic growth were not my priorities. But now, my focus was to quickly grow in terms of position and money which can get me recognition in society. With my changed focus, it was the perfect opportunity for me. With that understanding, I got a new hope and zeal. I did further research and found that a Post-Graduation program in Computer Science is offered by the Institute of Engineering and Technology, Lucknow (one of the seven government engineering colleges in Uttar Pradesh.) I came to know that they are conducting an entrance exam for the same.

My cousin, Vivek Gaur, and some well-wishers also motivated me to attempt the IAS (Indian Administrative Services) examination. These are the most prestigious services. IAS officers carry the 'Super Achievers' status, having credibility, power, authority, and contribution to India. The three-stage IAS qualification exam regime (IAS Prelims-mains-Interview) is the toughest in India and only the best brains qualify for the same.

At that time, my state of mind, my confidence was dented besides, I wanted to quickly grow. Hence, I was keen for a career in Information Technology rather than a long and uncertain journey to give attempts at IAS. However, looking at the 'Super Achiever' tag, I was tempted to give it a try as well. I found that the prelim examination for IAS is scheduled after six months. I immediately zeroed down to two major subjects, that I needed to take, to appear in the exams. I opted for Physics and Anthropology. Physics because of the obvious reasons and Anthropology because, I was told it was relatively easier.

For the first time after the M.Sc. debacle, I had a retaliation plan now:

- Build a career in Information Technology line as the first preference "to quickly grow and earn money."
- Give an attempt at the IAS exam once and see how it goes. However, I was skeptical since, I had only six months to prepare.

The bad times made me realize who is my real well-wisher and who is not. Even in the worst situations, there is fantastic learning. I decided to move on and started my retaliation. 'The Rebel' in me was ready, to return the society, the same fuck that it gave to me. The only option was to prove myself by being materialistically successful.

I began my mission and applied to both– entrance exams for PG Degree in Computer Science in the Institute of Engineering and Technology, Lucknow as well as Indian Administrative Services Prelims exams. Now that I was clear about my future course of action, I immediately started preparations for both exams.

The PG degree in Computer Science entrance exams went very well and I got selected as part of the 30-seat program. I took a huge sigh of relief having secured my first preferred option. I was very happy about this option, especially, after learning the growth projections and the financial security it may give to me. I started preparing for the course.

The start date of the Computer Science program was after the IAS Prelim exams. I put my full undivided focus on the IAS prelims exam. However, I was more confident in Physics than in Anthropology. I gave exam and was quite happy with my attempt. I thought, I will crack it.

My program started in IET Lucknow for the PG program in Computer Science. The program was specially designed to cover the basics of Computer Science and Applications. The classes started and it was interesting to get introduced to 30 fellow students. Many students had joined the program after completing their masters in mathematics and physics, because they also knew the demand in the information technology industry and wanted to ride the wave of growth.

In the meantime, I got the shocking news that IAS prelims exams have been canceled. The reason given was that some of the papers got leaked and the Public Service Commission decided to cancel the IAS prelims exams and will shortly announce a new date for the re-exam of IAS prelims. This was disappointing, as I thought my papers had gone well and I had a chance to sail through in the prelims.

"Well, looks like the stars are playing their role, as was predicted by the astrologer," I told myself. A unique sense of disappointment and relief came to me. I felt disappointed as my paper had gone well and I thought, I had a chance. But I also felt relieved, as now I had a clear way forward plan – Focus only on the information technology route to success. I started putting everything in the program.

During my final semester project, I met a gentleman, Pradeep Kumar, at a get-together at my sister Madhurima and her husband Gopal Ji Sinha's house. Pradeep Kumar is the husband of Gopal Ji's sister Sonia. Pradeep Kumar had completed graduation and post-graduation from IIT Kanpur and was heading the information technology division of Raymond Cement Works based in Bilaspur, Madhya Pradesh. I told him about my computer science program and my urge to grow fast due to my past situation.

Pradeep Kumar (PK) gave me a very valuable advice.

"IT industry is really growing and all companies are focusing on computerization and automation and hence there is a good demand of IT resources. So, getting a job should not be a problem. However, if you really want to grow faster, you need to focus on specialization in the latest technologies which are in great demand. For example, nowadays talents with command on UNIX, C, UNIFY are in great demand and these technologies seem to have a good future as well. Do some advanced course on these technologies and after completing your Computer Science program join my team in Raymond Cements Works at Bilaspur MP," he advised and offered me.

This was new learning that there are two different ways to rise:

1. **Ride the wave of new opportunities** concerning the industry. Like, I learned about the opportunities in Information Technology
2. **Ride the wave of specialization** (newer in-demand technologies)

This became one of the most important learning in my life. "This seems to be very valuable advice and I am going to follow the same. I will look forward to joining and working with you as soon as I complete the advanced specialization course," I humbly thanked him for his advice and happily agreed to join him after the course. Now, I had the assured offer in hand. I did my research and found that a six months specialized course is offered, on Unix, C and Unify, by one of the leading computers learning organizations of that time, UPTRON Advance Computer Learning. I immediately enrolled in that program. I completed the PG program in Computer Science and thereafter six months advanced specialization course in UNIX, C, UNIFY.

I received the offer letter even before the completion of the advanced specialization program stating to join Raymond Cement Work after I complete the advanced program. There was a huge sense of relief for me, my parents, and real well-wishers who stood by me.

"The journey to bounce back has started with the first break" I reminded myself.

The public service commission announced exams for some key positions, and though, I had already found my path, yet I decided to give the exams anyways, as I had prepared for IAS prelims. I was told the result will come after a few months. I was looking forward to my first job at Raymond, so after giving the exam I forgot about it.

Chapter 5

My retaliation had started

"Hello aunty, I am Sudeep," after a lot of thought, and with great anxiety and guts, I called Kalpana's mother.

There was no response from the other side.

I was a rebel but my love remained my weakness. I was on a retaliation path but now I had a job. I was fighting my battle to bounce back with a feeling of *Junoon* (passion) and with the right direction and break, I felt being on the right path. I felt positive with a ray of hope. But there was one unresolved thing that was bothering me which was "my image of a betrayer in the mind of Kalpana's mother." The more I thought about it, the more, I felt her feeling was justified. Any parent will feel betrayed under the given circumstances. She discovered my affair with Kalpana without the details of what exactly happened behind the scene— my actual intent, control, and resolve. I was very uncomfortable about this as it was not giving the right picture, and with half knowledge, it was questioning my intent. After a long thought and deliberation, I decided to call Kalpana's mother directly and clarify to her as to what exactly happened and what are my thoughts and intent now.

"Hello aunty, are you there?" I said once again.

"Hello," she finally replied with a stern tone.

"Aunty, I wanted to talk to you, please give me a few minutes. I have been feeling very bad and I want to clarify some things," I said.

"How can you do that? We trusted you. She is just a child," she sounded very angry and upset.

"I never planned this, aunty. You know very well how important was my higher studies and this was a distraction. But it did happen despite my trying to avoid it," I said with tears flowing and throat choked.

"But please trust me that I never tried to do anything wrong. I have never crossed my boundary. In fact, I have always emphasized the importance of our studies to Kalpana and made it a point that we cannot distract ourselves. You must have seen she is also focusing on studies seriously," I continued.

"This is not the age to get involved in such things. This is just not right and acceptable to us. You have broken our trust," she still was very angry and sounded hurt.

"My intentions are very pure aunty," I broke down and said in a choking voice "I want to marry your daughter and not take advantage of her. This is not a deception at all. And this is why I was further focusing on my studies and building a career," I emphasized.

"You still cannot do that as there is a big age gap between both of you." She still was very angry, but I felt that her anger had toned down. Kalpana was eight years younger than me and when I had told her this in our initial days of interaction, she had told me that even her parents have a major age difference.

"Aunty, there are many couples who have a little larger gap in their age. Even there is an age difference between you and uncle, so how does this matter?" I replied to her objection.

"How dare you talk about us? I just told you this is not right and that's it," she did not take my response well and became very angry again.

I immediately realized that I made a big mistake by comparing their age difference with ours. I just lost some gains that I had made.

"I am sorry aunty; I did not mean to upset you. Please tell me what shall I do now?" I pleaded with her in a crying voice with tears flowing.

There was a pause. I was trying to cope with my emotions.

"You just focus on building your career. Once you are in a good position and my daughter's age is also appropriate then we will talk about it. But in the meanwhile, you have to promise me that neither you will tell her about this discussion nor will you meet her. You will have to stop this immediately," she said after some deliberations.

I paused for a moment to process what she had just said.

Firstly, at least she is not saying 'No' forever which is a good thing, secondly, she is right that I must focus on my career. I can surely keep our talks a secret from Kalpana. But, I did not feel good about not meeting Kalpana till 'her age is right' and 'my career gets in a good shape' because this would mean waiting for at least 4-5 years.

I was in love and had seen the 'Maine Pyar Kiya' movie around 12 times. I remembered all the dialogues by heart. And to me, her conditions, sounded exactly like, what the father of Bhagyashree (heroine) demanded in the movie. In the moment of emotion, I decided to follow her advice with a slight request.

"Ok aunty, I will do what you say. I will focus on building my career. But not talking to her will be impossible and she will doubt my intentions. I promise that I will not meet her often and keep away the talks of love and instead focus our discussions on her studies and my career. And I will come back to you after establishing and proving myself," I told her in an emotional yet obediently convincing tone.

"And, you have to promise me that you will not talk about our discussions to her at all," she demanded conclusively.

"Ok aunty, I promise," I genuinely promised, crossing my heart.

There was a lull from both sides with a feeble sound of a sigh.

"Thanks, aunty, Namaste," I said and waited. And heard a phone disconnection sound from the other side.

"Oh boy, did I just have the guts to talk to Kalpana's mother?" I thought with disbelief but some relief and satisfaction. The communication gap and unknown feelings were bothering me for quite some time now, and I was quite relieved that, at least, I have broken that barrier. I had been feeling very bad that I have broken their trust, hence this was like bam, on that feeling. However, I knew that way forward is going to be tough and I have to follow my promise honestly to regain their trust and eliminate the feeling of guilt. Or

I thought that none of this would have happened if I would have been successful in M.Sc. engineering. This discussion further strengthened the revelation that being materialistically successful is very important. My resolve to come back faster and sooner became much stronger. I was happy that I am going to a different city, so that I can focus on building my career and not have my moments of weaknesses.

I WAS READY TO GO.

This was my first relocation outside my home since I never lived in a hostel. My mother was a little excited to see me getting a direction and yet emotional to send me away for the first time. I was told that I will be allotted a hostel room which is built for bachelors at Raymond. I planned, prepared, and said goodbye and left for Raymond Cement Works, Bilaspur, Madhya Pradesh.

Bilaspur, also known as "The City of Festivals", is a city located in undivided Madhya Pradesh (Now part of the carved-out state of Chhattisgarh.) This city is the commercial center and business hub of the region. It is very rich in minerals and there are many industries and mines around, like Coalfields, power plants, cement ore, and factories. It is also surrounded by many backward villages still untouched unlike the major development in urban areas of the country. Many cement factories were in the surrounding areas like ACC and Raymond.

I started my first long train journey from Lucknow to Bilaspur which crossed Bundelkhand and entered Madhya Pradesh and crossed through some dense forests and grasslands. The landscape in southern MP (now Chhattisgarh) indeed is beautiful, untouched, lush-green, and full of vegetation. You can see the jungle, mountains, high train bridges, and many amazing waterfalls. I loved traveling but this was for a new beginning for me with a new hope.

Raymond Cement Works was located around 40 kilometers away from Bilaspur town. The complete facility was developed over a large area located off the main highway and was known as Gopal Nagar. The facility consisted of a cement mining field, a cement processing factory, administrative buildings, a residential township, a shopping area for essential household materials, a research and development facility, and an area where they had plants and dairy.

Chapter 6

A New Beginning

"I heard you are working long hours and have worked continuously in the office for the last two days?" Pradeep Kumar asked me.

"Yes. There are two reasons, one, I have a lot to learn so want to spend as much time as I can and, two, I am away from home around Holi for the first time so wanted to indulge in work so that I don't feel homesick," I gave him an honest reply.

"Ok, come along with us to Holi celebrations within the township and later meet me so that I can give you some useful tips," he told me.

"Sure, I will," I said in a thankful voice.

Earlier last month, after reaching Raymond Cement Works, I had met Mr. Pradeep Kumar, Head of IT and Consulting Division, and thanked him for his invaluable advice about specialization and offering the first job of my life. After completing the joining formality, I was introduced to the management team with three seniors, Prasanna, Barin Roy, and Aryender Sharma. I was assigned to Prasanna and started learning my tasks without losing any time. It was a small and niche IT team and hence, I got the opportunity to learn many things at the same time. The first was to understand system administration activities like servers, backups, etc. For the first time, I saw big computer systems, large machines in the server room. I was taught how to take backups on large magnetic tapes. I also started working on database tasks.

My knowledge of Unix, C, and UNIFY, due to the specialization, came very handy. I was eager to learn, curious to apply my knowledge practically, and excited about the exposure to systems operations. My urge and hunger to grow faster was very high and I wanted to take more workload and learn as much as possible in a very short time. I started working at the level of *Junoon*. More work demanded more time from me, especially since I was new to the job. But that was no problem for me as I was away from home. I was satisfied that I am learning specialized technologies, which are much in demand in the market, as well as their practical application in the professional world. I started working for long hours, 16-18 hours at times. Even when, I used to go back to take a rest, I used to have manuals, books, notes to read and learn from. I was getting fantastic support from my leaders. Occasionally, during the weekends or late nights, Mr. Prasanna, being a fun person, used to call for a beer party, which used to be pretty wild with drink, food, and dance themes. I learned the technique of "dancing till you sweat." It used to take away my pain of rejection by society and being far away from my love, used to give me much-needed rejuvenation at times. But like a hungry bear, my focus was very much to learn more and more.

I had joined Raymond in February 1991, and after around a month of working, I was well accepted in the work environment. I was working madly to prove myself. Then came the festival of Holi, in March, and I felt a little homesick. To suppress this feeling, I decided to spend time working in the office. I spent two days in the office continuously and came back early morning on the day of the Holi festival. Mr. Pradeep Kumar came to know about this and had called me to know about this.

Later, I got ready and celebrated Holi along with the colleagues of Raymond Cement Works (RCW). The good part of such a township is that everyone lives away from their native places, and that makes them live like a big family. I was told that all festivals like Holi are celebrated with good fun, together.

Holi was a daylong celebration with food, fun, games around a nearby picnic spot. I felt really good as it gave a family-like feeling after almost a month. After Holi, I went back again to my insane 16-18 hours work schedule. I was happy that I was learning fast and my managers were happy too. I remembered, that PK had also asked me to meet him, as he wanted to give me some advice, so I approached him one day.

"You had asked me to meet you regarding some advice/tips that you wanted to give me," I reminded him.

"Oh yes. Are you still working long hours?" He asked me.

"Yes, but I am enjoying it," I gave my honest answer.

"What about your sleep, are you sleeping well?" He again asked.

"I am fine with 5 hours of sleep," I replied.

"Meet me today at lunchtime and we will talk about it," he told me.

"Sure, I will come. Thanks," I nodded.

I met him later in the day and we went to his home after lunch.

"Do you know anything about *Yog Nidra* or 'Power nap'?" He asked.

"I have not heard about *Yog Nidra* but I have seen my dad taking 'Power nap' effectively sitting anywhere," I said with a little confusion and curiosity while smiling thinking about dad's habit of quick naps.

"Let me introduce you to the Yog Nidra, a technique which will rejuvenate you within 30 minutes as if you have slept for hours," he spoke.

This was surprising for me and at the same time, I was very curious as this can be a solution to sustained hard work without getting tired.

PK gave me a little brief about Yog Nidra. Also known as yogic sleep, it is a powerful technique for controlling your body's relaxation response. Yog Nidra can be as restorative as sleep, while you remain fully conscious. Cultivate conscious relaxation, ease ongoing stress and anxiety, and feel your body melt away into a soothing state of being. It is a systematic practice of moving awareness from the external world to the inner world. It brings us to a state of deep sleep where our senses, intellect, and mind relax. After closing the doors and switching off the lights he inserted the Yog Nidra cassette in his jukebox.

"Let's lie down flat on the carpet with our back on the ground and face facing the ceiling," he asked me to do that. I followed his instructions.

"Close your eyes and listen carefully to what is instructed in the cassette," he said. I closed my eyes and started listening carefully.

Soothing light music played on cassette and a voice started instructions:

1. *Focus on relaxing the body completely.*

   This was said for a few minutes.

2. *Then the instructions were to focus on breathing in various ways.* By now my body started feeling quite relaxed

3. *Then the instructions started repeating to focus on each finger, the palm, back of the hand, hand as a whole, forearm, elbow, upper arm, shoulder joint, shoulder, neck, each section of the face (forehead, eyes, nose, and so on), ear, scalp, throat, chest, rib cage, shoulder, waist, stomach, abdomen, buttocks, thigh, top and back of the knee, calf, ankle, top of foot, heel, toes,* etc.

4. *Then the voice said to focus on the whole body. And then again to different body parts of another side.* By now after repeating this for some time, I could visualize my body in my mind and felt very relaxed. Within a few minutes, I started feeling like I am seeing my body from above.

5. *The voice said to focus on the surrounding space around the body.*

   By this time, I felt like floating in the room. And suddenly, I got scared as I was floating above the body and the fan was running in the room. In that state, for a moment, I got worried that I may get hit by a fan. I tried hard to keep floating away from the fan.

6. *Then I heard the voice instructing me to return to consciousness.*

   Slowly, I lost the vision of floating and felt inside my body lying flat on the carpet.

7. *Then I heard the voice instructing me to Gently move my fingers for a few moments, take a deep breath, and then open my eyes slowly.*

   As instructed, I slowly started moving my hand fingers and then hand and then leg and then slowly opened my eyes.

I felt like, I had slept for hours whereas when I looked at the clock, I realized the whole process took only around 40 minutes. My body was feeling so relaxed and rejuvenated. This was the first time in my life I was experiencing something which was beyond my imagination. I clearly remembered the feeling of floating in the air and seeing my body lying on the floor. I had been a science student and looked for evidence, logic in everything and here, I experienced something which I couldn't understand. I was aware of the basic concept, that the soul resides in the body and after death, it leaves the body. And that the Rishi-Muni (Holy Men) had gained the power of taking the soul out and travel in different times and come back (they used to be called Trikal-darshi, one who can see various times – past and future). But neither had I seen any such holy man nor did I think that one can come out of the body with just 30 minutes of instructions of Yog Nidra. I was a little confused with my current experience – a mixed feeling of hitting a jackpot plus wondering if it was just a dream. After that day, I started practicing Yog Nidra quite often as I was curious and wanted to experience it again. I was loving the feeling of rejuvenation even after spending long hours working.

After two months, I got an independent house shared by one more colleague. This was a two-bedroom, drawing-dining room house with a big backyard. I was very happy with my first house. Now, I had the opportunity to study, cook and practice Yog Nidra in solitude.

One day, I was doing Yog Nidra and as usual, after a few steps, I started floating in the room but got worried about the rotating ceiling fan and came back quickly out of Yog Nidra. Awake, I reasoned with myself that if the soul is just a form of energy, then it shall not worry about getting harmed by a fan or any other objects. The next time when I meditated, I switched off the fan and performed Yog Nidra. This time I was not worried about the fan but curiously tried to touch the fan while floating in the air, and realized that I could not touch the fan blades. When I came back from Yog Nidra, I realized that I need not worry about any object in the room as the soul is just pure energy.

My office work was going on at full speed and I was happy that my body was also relaxed with Yog Nidra despite less sleep. I thought this is going perfectly well as my learning is not getting impacted by body fatigue. One day, I completed my walk in the township which had a beautifully carved lawn in the shape of the map of India. The map was quite big and so from a visual perspective, it was not fully visible from the inclination at which the pathway was laid. I wondered how it may look from above. I had decided to try to come out of the home during the Yog Nidra, and see the park, floating above it.

I started the usual practice following steps and quickly started floating. Then, I tried to go out of the room. But somehow, I was not able to go out of the room as there were walls and I did not know how to pass through the walls. I desperately tried but did not succeed. I came out of the session and was a little disappointed but thought maybe it is not possible. After that, I did not try to go out of the room.

Summers came and by now, I was assigned additional work in the payroll application team with Mr. Sharma. I learned the detailed process of time cards, timesheets, and how that was taken as input for payroll and other details. This was the first time, I started interacting with our end customers, the Human Resources team. I was enthusiastic and started putting my heart and soul into understanding the process, application, customer needs, and customer behavior. I felt satisfied and happy with the learning. Time was flying by, with my passion for work, and the newfound habit of Yog Nidra.

A batch of fresh engineers joined our team and soon we became good friends. We started learning more and more as well as we started exploring areas nearby Bilaspur. We used to take the Raymond bus during the weekends that used to go to Bilaspur town and used to have fun watching movies and dining outside. The fun quotient had increased. And, I started living in a 'Work hard Party harder' mode. But I named it **'Excellence with Fun.'** Often, the park used to be our get-together place.

One day, I came back from the park and I decided to practice Yog Nidra. Within 10 minutes, I was floating and was very relaxed. And in that state of relaxed floating, I just remembered about the park where we were a few minutes back. Suddenly, I found myself floating above the park. I was surprised as well as delighted. "How did this happen?" I asked myself without getting any answers in that state of floating. I started enjoying the view of the park and saw the map of India with a full view floating on the top. This was a new view for me that I had not seen earlier. I heard some noise and slowly came back from Yog Nidra. Someone was ringing the bell and that broke my concentration.

When I got free later that night, I started thinking about what had happened and about the view of the park while floating over it. But there was no way I could have validated if that is the view in reality, as there was no real view of the park from elevation, even from any higher buildings nearby. I wondered, if that was my imagination and left it to that. But this gave me a perspective that I can venture out as well.

"Can I travel to Lucknow and see my family and friends?" a question came to my mind. "Well, why not, there is nothing wrong in trying," I comforted myself. I decided and started trying to go to Lucknow. But a very funny thing happened to me. In the Yog Nidra session, I reached Bilaspur railway station and boarded the train but when the train started moving, I remained in the same place while the train left. I even tried to run after the train on the tracks to catch it but saw the train going out of my vision. I wanted to see my family and Kalpana and I was disappointed at my failure. However, I decided not to give up. And then it happened in one of the Yog Nidra sessions wherein the state of floating and boarding the train, I just remembered Lucknow, and I saw myself floating in the corridors outside Universal Book Shop in Hazratganj (Lucknow's main shopping area of the time). That building has old construction of round pillars in front of corridors and the shops inside. One such shop is the Universal Book Shop, which is one of my favorite places. It was a feeling of divinity and happiness with which I was gliding smoothly between the pillars. I just loved it. Then I started floating above the Hazratganj main road reaching Sahu theater, one of the posh movie halls in Lucknow. In that state of floating, I just wondered what would it be like on the top of the Sahu theatre. And, I floated above the building and saw the constitution of that place which I had never seen earlier. Even in that state of floating it was a unique view and experience. I heard some noise and came out of the session.

I felt a little disappointed that after great practice, I finally reached Lucknow but came back without meeting family due to a break in concentration. However, I also felt extremely happy to have reached Lucknow and with the divine experience of floating in Hazratganj. Since, I had not seen the top of Sahu theatre earlier, I could not validate the same and I thought it must be my imagination and left it to that. I was happy and had hope that now I may be able to see my loved ones. With restrictions due to my promise given to Kalpana's mother, I did not want to create more spark and desperation in my love life. I had called Kalpana only twice since I came five months back. I told her that I am working very hard for our future and she should also focus on her studies.

But now, with the success of reaching Lucknow in Yog Nidra, I became greedier to see her and my family. So, I kept on trying. And as they say, *'Kehte hain agar kisi cheez ko dil se chaho, to puri kainat use tumse milane ki koshish me lag jati hai"* meaning *"If you love something from heart, then all of the universe conspires to help you getting that."* And that is exactly what happened with me next. *After trying in a few sessions, I succeeded in reaching my house and saw my mother in our house in Lucknow. I was delighted to see her sitting in her bed. Then I moved to Kalpana's house but did not see anyone there. She was not there.* I felt delighted to see my mother after a long time.

And then in the next session, I saw her, my little thing, my Kalpana. She was sitting at her desk in her room. She wore a blue skirt and a white top. I was so happy to see her studying. Even in that floating situation, I felt a sweet pain in my heart, "Oh man, how much have I missed her." I was there in that room for some time, watching her face. I wanted to tell her that I am there next to her but I could not because I was in that floating energy state. I heard a knock on my door and came back. I could not sleep that night and was very restless and helpless the next day. "What am I doing? Why I cannot be with her? Why do people have to see materialistic status to accept you? I felt miserable. But now, I had tasted blood and I wanted more. So, the next day, I did not go to the office thinking I will have completely undisturbed and focused time alone at home. I tried again.

She wore her college uniform and was talking to someone on phone in the drawing-room. She seemed happy. I felt delighted seeing her happy as that's all I wanted to see. After a few minutes, she hung the phone and walked to her room, and closed the door. I came along, floating. She opened her almirah and took out some clothes and threw them on the bed. Then she went to her table and opened a book and started turning some pages. I was very emotional thinking she is focusing on her studies. And then she closed the windows and picked up her clothes to change. Even in that state, I felt a sensation and a mixed feeling of 'Oh wow' and 'Oh shit'. 'Is this right?' 'NO!'– a strong voice came from my inner self and I floated outside her room in the balcony. And then in a few seconds, I found myself back, floating in my room. I got up finding myself drenched in sweat. I was restless and started talking to myself.

"What did happen just now? I was watching her, but she was not aware of it. Is this not an intrusion of privacy?" I questioned myself. "Well, I was just trying to see her and not make intrusion of her privacy", I tried to justify. "But if you would have stayed there, what would have happened? Your, watching her normally is fine but what about her private space? Would she be comfortable if she knew I was watching?" I thought from her perspective. "No, she won't," I realized.

"Then does going to see her unannounced, would not intrude on her privacy? What if, when I go there and she is already in her private space/ situation?" I was trying to find sense now.

"Yes. I would not know what she is doing when I am trying to reach her, whether it is her private moment or not. So, I may end up intruding on her personal space despite my intention not to do so," I now have understood the bigger danger. If I would have done that with her consent then it would still have been ok. The recent craziness to see her had impacted my work, taking me away from my objective.

"I must stop it as this is wrong. I may end up intruding personal space of my loved ones without intention. This is addictive and I am losing focus from my biggest purpose– my retaliation to prove my worth and get to a respectable position quickly," I reasoned and concluded.

It indeed was a hard decision but I had realized it was wrong for my value system and objective. Despite having the right intention, the situation and the process, one cannot know another person's situation.

I avoided practicing Yog Nidra and instead indulged heavily in work, overloading myself, so that I don't get time to think at all.

PK summoned me to his room urgently. I wondered what happened?

Chapter 7

"Have you applied for any other job?" PK asked me.

"No. Why do you ask?" I was surprised at the question.

"Are you sure, you are not interested in any other job?" He probed.

"Not at all. I am getting to learn a great deal out here. I am so thankful to you for everything starting from the advice to do specialization, offering a job, and giving me a tremendous platform to learn and grow here. And of course, the Yog Nidra practice which has helped me tremendously," I responded with gratitude. I had not told him about my Yog Nidra ventures recently.

"Well, your father called and said you have been selected in the public service commission exam that you gave," he announced.

"Oh God!" I exclaimed. I had completely forgotten about that exam which I had given casually before leaving Lucknow to join Raymond. "My sincere apologies, I gave that exam very casually along with some friends, before even joining Raymond. And in fact, I had completely forgotten about that. Neither was, I sure, I would qualify nor did, I remember that," I told in a humble and apologetic language. He listened to me curiously looking at my changed facial expressions.

"I am so happy learning and growing here that I am not going to accept this offer anyways. That is a government job and I have heard that learning and growth happens much faster in the private sector, especially in the information technology space," I gave my logic.

"That is true. But your father was sounding very happy and excited about you cracking the public service commission exam. And I believe, he wants you to join that," he shared his discussion with my father.

"Well, I am very sure. I want to continue here," I was very firm.

"Let us talk to your father later today," he concluded the discussion.

I came back to my desk and started processing the new information. I felt happy that I qualified for that exam. At the same time, I could see that there is tremendous growth in information technology in the private sector. What is my ultimate objective, I thought? To grow fast (Speed of growth), get a respectable position (Position & Respect), and earn money (Financially very strong.) Together this will make me materialistically successful. I did not know anything about the offer and posting in the selection letter, so while I was firm in my mind to stay back yet, I wanted to know the details from my father.

"This is public services commission which means it is a government job and the pay scale is also very good which means it is a very respectable beginning in the government," my father was excited.

"But Papa, I am very happy here. I am learning a lot in a very short time which is good for my faster growth. Only the private sector can give such growth and I desperately want to grow fast. Besides work environment here is very good," I was firm in my logic.

"The letter says you are given the position in the World Bank Monitoring Cell at the Secretariate in Lucknow. This is a very big break. I know many IAS officers there as well as ministers with whom I have worked," he replied in a tone questioning my ignorance.

"But Papa…" I was trying to reply.

"Do you know how difficult it is to get a government job and that too a respectable one with nice placement, location, grade, and package? It will be foolish to even think about leaving this. No more discussions, you are coming back here!" he kept on saying without noticing that I was trying to say something. He was a little upset at my insistence.

"Sorry Papa, but I am staying back here," I gave my firm decision.

He disconnected the phone. I was not sure if he heard my last sentence but it looked to me like he had heard me.

"I told my dad that I am staying back here," I told PK later.

He smiled and asked, "Are you sure? Is your dad convinced?"

"I am sure. But, dad was very much enchanted with the perks of a government job as he had been a government servant and does not know the potentials of the private sector since he has not seen that part of the world," I told him genuinely.

"Good then, continue with your work," he smiled and patted my back.

PK is my true mentor, who saved my life with his fantastic advice which has helped me tremendously. Despite being such a towering personality holding such a senior position, he has been humble, approachable, and helpful. I am indebted and want to work with him.

"Your father is coming here tomorrow to take you back," PK told me.

"What? Oh God!" I was totally surprised to hear that.

"Looks like he is determined," he smiled at me.

"I don't want to go and don't know what else to say," I responded.

"Let him come and we will talk to him," He spoke.

He gave me **another valuable piece of advice** "Have you done your **pros-con analysis between the two options you have**? It is always **better to take well, thought through decisions**

instead of emotional ones." He made sense. Decisions taken without deliberation may cause regret or pain later.

"I have given a quick thought but, I will think it through in detail with pros and cons. After that, I will discuss this with you," I assured him.

I started thinking:

Current Job:

- Pros: Private sector - Demanding job; Opportunities to learn quickly; Higher growth in Information technology; Reach destination quickly; Focus more on work being away from home.
- Cons: Location; fewer options; No performance – No growth.

World Bank offer:

- Pros: Secured and stable government job; Location; Reputed job; World Bank placement
- Cons: Slower growth; Difficult to focus; Lesser opportunities

The experience of the past seven months had been very good.

"Though the exact nature of work in the World Bank opportunity is not clear on papers, this does not look bad. Look at the keywords – Government, World Bank, Information Technology, and the capital town of Lucknow. This sounds good," PK heard and reasoned. Father came and all arguments were subsided as he insisted.

"Why don't you try it and if you do not like then join back," PK offered.

The decision was made. I was going back to Lucknow to take the job at World Bank. Overall, I was apprehensive, but deep inside, I was happy.

Chapter 8

World Bank Monitoring Cell consisted of five persons – Principal Secretary, Special Secretary, Joint Secretary, Officer on Special Duty (OSD), and Technical Lead/Programmer (myself). The first three were senior IAS officers whereas OSD was a very senior non-IAS official. So, most of them were almost double my age except the joint secretary, who was around 10 years senior to me. This was a sea change for me after Raymond. Raymond was a remote location, a very open and spacious place with modern architecture. Whereas, the Lucknow Secretariate was a wonderful state government headquarter building but still congested and old. I was initially allocated under the leadership of OSD. Since, I was the only technical person with the knowledge of computers and the rest were all senior bureaucrats, they gave me free hand to do what I want to do. I asked about the work and I was told that there is a huge World Bank grant and we need to manage and monitor the use of that fund for the uplifting the technical education in the state of Uttar Pradesh. Scope included all engineering colleges and polytechnics in the state. This was a huge task as everything was done manually till now. This meant that I needed to automate all the processes and then monitor the progress.

I started everything from the scratch, from getting computers, software, printer, to understanding the monitoring process and then developing the software application. I immediately realized that in a government office everything goes slow, BUT if one wants to push, then being the power center, things can move quite quickly. I took this power to my advantage and got the required systems arranged quickly, on loan, from the engineering colleges, as they were the recipient of the funds.

I met Kalpana and there were a lot of emotions from both sides. We indeed had missed each other. But I had controlled my emotions as I still knew that my targeted destination is still a few years away besides, I still remembered the promise I made to her mother. But, I was very happy and drowned in love. It was difficult to suppress feelings in this state of mind. Towards the end of our meeting, I told her that I still need to grow fast to give my proper response to society. While she knew the rebel in me but was not able to comprehend why I am still upset. And yes, I was still very hurt by what had happened to me.

On the way back, I was passing through Hazratganj and saw Sahu Theater. I remembered the Yog Nidra session where I had floated above Sahu Theater and had seen a distinctive structure that I had never seen earlier. Though I had dismissed the 'incidence as a possible imagination' but I was curious to see how it is in reality. I thought to check it out. The rooftop was locked, but I got hold of someone and went to the rooftop. As I reached the rooftop, I was stunned.

"Oh My God!" I exclaimed and went speechless watching that view. It was exactly the same, that I had seen during the Yog Nidra session.

I got goosebumps and was literally shivering in disbelief.

"Does that mean that all I saw in the state of floating during Yog Nidra was true?" Immediately, this question came to my mind.

I had more faith now in the power of Yog Nidra. After all, this Yogic technique is not just about relaxation but there is much more.

"Thank God! I did not breach anyone's privacy. I was just lucky to be floating and seeing people when they were not in their private space," the scary thought came. I reaffirmed to stop practicing it.

At work, I evaluated the situation and realized that I need to go back to my *Junoon* mode. For the next three months, I put my head down to understand the monitoring process and started developing the automation software program. I came out with a test version of the application and informed my OSD. He advised me to show it to the special secretary. I was allocated two seats, one was sharing the room with the OSD, and the second sharing with the special secretary. I explained the same to the special secretary.

"This sounds like fantastic work. Does this work fully?" the special secretary complimented and probed me.

"It is as per the process I have understood, but first, I need to run a pilot on this application to find any gaps and fix them," I proposed.

"Ok, let's do that immediately," he seemed happy and asked his assistant to call for a meeting with all senior leaders of the technical education department who were dealing with the World Bank Project. After his briefing in the meeting, we decided to start running the pilot of the application, in a limited manner.

Besides minor process gaps, the application was found to be running fine. I fixed the gaps and it started working fine. This brought me in the limelight as all secretaries were happy about it and even the principal secretary complimented me. I felt very confident and fulfilled. This indeed was a big achievement, also because I worked primarily on my own without any technical support.

The next few months were busy in the monitoring activities and creating projections, monitoring progress, and status reviews. This brought me in direct touch with all the Directors of the engineering colleges and polytechnics. And since they needed funds and wanted their progress to be right in front of secretaries, they started cajoling me. Suddenly, I became very popular, internally and externally.

The recognition of my work, the importance of my role, my proximity with secretaries, and being the only person with IT expertise made me the center of attraction. The technical education department staff was appreciating my work, as the ease of operation was helping them. Since, I used to work on computers, secretaries also tried to understand the same from me. I had all the facilities like a phone with an international call facility. A lot of time, I used to travel in office car to various facilities alone or along with bureaucrats. And whenever a policeman, gave a salute to a 'Blue beacon' car on the crossings, I used to feel very good (especially at that stage of my career). I used to feel important and recognized. My career was on track and I felt good.

Since, I was deeply in love and was not able to meet Kalpana as frequently, I used to feel low. One day, my fast friend Amit (Shalabh Rastogi), took me to watch the new movie 'Lamhe' starring Sridevi and Anil Kapoor in Sahu theater for a 12 PM-3 PM show. That movie touched me so much that after the movie, I just did not want to move out of the theater. I told Amit to please get me the next show ticket. We saw the next show and again I cried, watching the movie. After the second show, we watched the movie continuously for the third time.

One day, me and Amit, decided that we will watch as many movies as we can in a day, in the movie hall. We watched five movies back-to-back in the movie hall – Ghost, Jo Jeeta Wohi Sikandar, Mera Naam Joker, Deewana & Khiladi. We ran from one picture hall to another, and by the end of the day, we were exhausted but laughed heartily.

The second half of 1992

After developing and implementing the applications, I started regular monitoring. It was more of management and administrative work for me for a few months. I started feeling empty as, I was not getting new work. I thought "although, I am enjoying it now, but what next? Will I not grow obsolete without latest computer application knowledge?" This thought scared me. I started wondering what to do next.

"**STAY HUNGRY, FOCUSED & CONTINUE CLIMBING**," I told myself.

"Boss, I am not learning anything new," I told my special secretary.

"But you are doing good work, everyone is happy with you and your automation is helping in bringing speed and efficiency," he was surprised by my question.

"Thank you, Boss, for recognizing my work and being supportive. But I am restricted to only administrative, management, and monitoring work. My skills on computer applications are going down as I don't have much to develop here," I gave him my reason of dissatisfaction.

"Do you want to do anything else here?" he was curious.

"I don't have any idea of what else can be done here. But in my first job at Raymond, I had a lot of work, learning, and hence enriched knowledge, and I am missing that. I was thinking of going back to the private sector," I told him hesitantly.

"What are you saying? You want to quit this wonderful government job?" he sounded surprised and a little upset. Then he paused for a second and said again with a mild smile "You are already doing good and I can see good growth possibilities for you. Do not take any decision emotionally and arbitrarily. Go back and think through. Anyways, I will not let you go. Let us talk about it next week."

Though, I felt happy with his appreciation and confidence showed in me, yet I still felt disappointed as I did not see my future here. I went back home and shared with my father, the conversations I had with the special secretary. My father was more upset with me.

"I don't know why you are not understanding the importance of a government job. And by the way, I talked to your special secretary, a few days back, and he was very happy with your work. Why do you want to destroy all the good work and fantastic job?" he asked.

"Yes, I am in limelight because of the work I have done so far. But, I see stagnation in terms of real hands-on work. In the IT field, technology is changing at a very fast pace and if I will not keep learning newer things with hands-on practice then my knowledge will soon become outdated. Right now, it is all just nuisance value without any real work. My creative side is not getting utilized. The special secretary was asking me what else I want to do but I don't see much scope in the World Bank monitoring cell," I spoke.

"Then think what else you want to do, and with the power of these senior bureaucrats, if they see value in what else you want to do, then they will support and help you," he spoke.

I thought about it but could not think. The next day the Director of the Institute of Engineering and Technology, Lucknow, visited our office and I was talking to him about my frustration and he offered me "Why don't you come to the engineering college and join the Computer Science department for some time? You can work on many things including helping final year students on their final projects which will include many ideas on latest technologies." I thought it's a good idea. I went to the special secretary and shared with him my possible interest in helping engineering college final year students on their projects as well as take some sessions.

He was happy with this option and thought that at least I am staying back within the department. He called engineering college directors and within a matter of few days, I was given the appointment letter of Bundelkhand Engineering College, Jhansi. I was a little surprised about the offer from BEC, Jhansi instead of IET Lucknow, but still happily took the offer as I thought, I will be working on the latest software and helping multiple projects.

I joined BEC, Jhansi in June'1992 and started helping students. I was very happy because there was so much work, classes, labs, projects and on top of that the respect of the students. I was given a house on campus, and since I was single, I opted for food in the canteen along with the students. After the rains in September, I started facing huge health problems due to the canteen food. I tried for a few more months but my condition deteriorated. The news reached my special secretary of technical education and he called me in Lucknow.

"I have heard that you are facing health challenges?" He asked.

"Yes Boss, somehow my stomach is not able to cope up with the food there," I responded.

"Come back here, we need you back," he offered.

"I will be fine with that but what will I do here? I have one proposition for you. I have seen the work at the section level in each department in the secretariat. It is very difficult to track files, with whom it is, and for how long. And it is a painful thing for everyone. I want to develop a Model Computerized Department Section for Technical Education. And if it is successful then the same can be replicated for all other departments in the government secretariat," I offered him a good proposition. I was skeptical as this was a big thing, never done earlier.

He thought for a moment and then responded "Ok create a pilot project and if you can do this, then this will be a huge success."

"Thank you so much and I will give my best. But, I will need support from the people at the section level to understand their actual way of working," I further requested him.

"Done. All the best," he said and moved out for another meeting.

I was delighted as this was a big opportunity for me. Not only it will give me hands-on work but also the highest level of exposure in the department.

Chapter 9

I had found a new work to satisfy my hunger. I planned my approach to handle this opportunity to create a model technical education department section in the government secretariat:

1. Understand the current way of working (As-Is Process)
2. Understand the pain points and the need (The Gap)
3. Based on the need, propose improved process (To Be Process)
4. Then automate a new process to bring in the predictability (of file location) and efficiency (time taken to address an issue) etc.

With the instructions of the secretaries, I got the attention of all the stakeholders of the department section. I sat with various stakeholders and started understanding the current process, their pain points as well as what is the possible solution according to them (Later in my career, I learned that this is part of the famous **Kaizen process**, that the Japanese use very efficiently for process improvement). I realized that many times files get lost, as there is no track of their movement, from where to where it moved and when. I was really surprised to see the condition of the file room. No wonder it was common to face difficulties in finding a file and sometimes files were lost. I had understood additional pain points that were not told to me by section people, just by watching the process and condition. I noted all the points, and started creating a flow chart of the complete file movement process, and marked various points of concern as well as improvement. After I created the flow chart and the improvement points, I discussed the same with the section officer and took his inputs. I finalized a sample improved flow chart of the processes to show to the special secretary.

"Boss, the situation I saw is very grave and unfortunate," I told him and explained what I saw in the last few days. While, he knew some of it yet he too was surprised to hear the actual scenario on the ground.

"What is your plan now, how do you want to proceed?" He was eager.

"I want to start the automation in parts, and not in one go, as that may face resistance besides it will be too much to change in one instance. I want you to give a mandate for the process change as this will be a big change for people who had been working in a set manner for a long-time and may resist any change. This may also expose some non-performing people, so they may also resist. So, I will need your help to manage the resistance too," I shared the plan and requested.

'Sure, you got it," He agreed.

To create a model section for technical education, I first identified the file movement system and started creating an application for the same. The application was very simple. I finished the programming part and was ready for the pilot launch. I gave the demo to the secretaries and OSD and they were happy about it.

After about a week, the special secretary asked for a review of all important files. On the day of review, it was a blast. He saw that most of the files were behind schedule. He could now see with whom the file is and whether there is a delay. He wanted to set the tone right, so he blasted everyone on non-compliance. Everyone in the room was silent and I was sitting next to him seeing the reaction. After blasting everyone, he demanded that he needs people to take corrective action within 24 hours. People left taking the note. The special secretary told me that I have done a very good job and that this may change the system for betterment, as now accountability will be tracked and monitored. I was happy but at the same time, a little uncomfortable with the way he had talked to section people. The moment I went out of the meeting room, everyone started blaming me for what I have done, and that this application is the reason why they were blasted by the special secretary. I felt really bad and disappointed. I was only trying to make improvements. The result of that meeting was such that now everyone had started taking file movement seriously besides the completion of the work on time. In a few weeks and months situation became much better. I also started slowly taking people into confidence by showing how much time they are saving by this automation as well as reducing the time-wastage in locating files. Additionally, I requested a special secretary to encourage people to adopt. The application was well adopted.

I was awarded the appreciation for "Commendable and Excellent Quality Contribution" for consequently the second year by the seniors, including my special secretary. There was a special award given to me on "Preparing an efficient software to efficiently and quickly disposing of the pending cases." Additionally, he certified that I can be trusted for 'Secret' work in the government. This was a huge appreciation and motivation for me, as this had placed me in the inner trust circles of the leaders.

In the meanwhile, since I had received bonuses and I had good savings, I purchased my first motorcycle – Suzuki Samurai. This red color beauty became my best friend as this was my first major purchase from my savings without any loan from my father or anyone else. I had not been in contact with Kalpana, for some time, I tried to reach out to her, but unfortunately could not connect with her. I was very unhappy not to have met her for a couple of months now. I decided to complete the project and meet her in peace.

I started working on the wider computerization of the technical education department. I took other parts of my original flow charts, that I had created for overall improvement, and started creating applications step by step. I wanted to get the help of an additional person to program to speed up the progress and I was promised that I will get help from the engineering colleges.

The programmer and I divided the work. It took three months to build the comprehensive model section application for the technical education department. I gave the program demo to the OSD first and after his feedback, I was further approached by the special secretary for the demo. He saw the application and was pretty happy.

"Let us run this internally for a couple of months, and after it gets stabilized, and we have some data to showcase, we shall take it to the Chief Secretary of the government of Uttar Pradesh," he told me.

I was pretty happy and excited with the visibility of this application. As planned, I rolled out a small pilot of the application since we needed approval from the chief secretary to fully implement the same.

"I am getting closer to my target," I told myself.

I received a call from Supriya, the younger sister of my close friend, to meet her and take her to a movie. She was also a close friend of Kalpana and knew about our relationship very well. I gave my confirmation.

Chapter 10

We decided to go to a nearby movie hall from Supriya's house and after greetings, we went to see the movie "100 days" starring Madhuri Dixit and Jacky Shroff. I had known Supriya for many years since she was very young. She had been like my younger sister. But when I met her this time, she was a little serious, trying to give a fake smile, which I found a little awkward but could not be understood.

The movie started and we went deep into the story of the movie. And then came the interval. I brought snacks for her. As I sat down, she said in a serious voice.

"I need to tell you something," she spoke.

"I could tell that there is something different about your expressions today. Tell me, what is it?" I asked.

"I think you should look for someone better for you," she said softly.

"Sorry, but I did not understand what you are trying to say," I wanted to understand what she meant.

"Bhaiyya, you are doing well and there will be many more beautiful girls for you, so look for them," she said hesitantly.

This cam as surprising shock for me and I understood that there is a deeper meaning for this statement. Many people close to me who knew about my affair wanted me to move on but of course, I was very clear about my liking and choice. So, coming this time from her, it left me confused. I honestly thought she is trying to refer to someone else.

"Please tell me clearly, what do you want to say exactly," I urged her.

"Kalpana is seeing someone else," she said plainly as I had asked.

Booooooooom……

"What?" I could hardly utter a word.

"Yes, she has started seeing someone for a little while now," she said firmly, confirming once again.

I did not understand what has just happened and I just went blank. I don't remember what exactly happened to me but in that state of blankness, I must have come out of the movie theatre and walked miles without realizing where I am going. I actually did not cry or shout. I kept roaming on roads like a clueless person for hours. I reached home and went to my room and locked it. I just kept staring at walls and fans on the ceiling. By the time, I realized it was the next morning. I have no idea what happened between yesterday's movie and this morning. I did not sleep at all but did not remember what I thought. I was completely out of sense.

Mom knocked at my door and I opened it quietly. She asked me what has happened but I just ignored her, as if I had not heard her. There was a critical meeting planned along with my secretary but I just forgot and did not go to the office. Nothing was making sense to me. I did not want to be at home also in this frame of mind. I took my bike and went to a nearby jungle called Kukrail. I stopped my bike in the middle of the jungle and started talking to myself about what has just happened.

"This cannot happen. I am sure there is some misunderstanding."

"But the news is shared by my Supriya, who is Kalpana's best friend, so this cannot be completely wrong either."

"I have been avoiding Kalpana due to my promise to her mother. I think she may have misunderstood it as my ignorance of her."

"So, is this a way for her to show that she is angry with me? But she may not actually be seeing someone?"

"I must talk to her to find the truth."

"If this is a way to make me feel jealous then she has succeeded but I am very furious with her for this. She just cannot do that."

I tried to call her but every time the phone was picked by her mother, so, I did not speak and cut the phone. I was very restless as I did not have any other way to talk to her.

I called Supriya, to understand the matter more. She asked me to come home and I went to her home.

"What has happened, tell me the truth? I am breaking," I pleaded.

"There are many things. First, she thought you are avoiding her. You only talk about studies and not beyond that. But most importantly she had been having a difficult time at home. Her mom has very clearly told her that she can marry anyone except you," she told me. "She has been very frustrated. And then someone else has been pursuing her for some time so she just fell for it," she continued.

"I don't think it will work now and I think you also move on. That's why I was telling you that you can get many beautiful girls," she urged.

I felt completely shattered. I quietly walked out and went to Residency (Historical ruins in Lucknow which once served as the residence for the British Resident General) and sat down. I started talking to myself.

"Seven years of relationship is snapped just like that?"

"But, I also did not give enough time to her. Of course, she would have thought that I am not interested in her anymore."

"Then she should have at least asked me."

"Well, she did want to meet more but, I did not meet her as often. I also did not tell her why I am not meeting her and about my conversation with her mother. All I told her was that I am creating my career and when the time will come then we will take the next steps."

"But I was keeping my promise given to her mother. How could I have not followed the promise when she gave me hope. Besides, I would have never thought that, at this age, she will find someone else so quickly," I was very furious with this thought. I decided not to give up.

In the meanwhile, my principal secretary sent someone to my home to check my wellbeing as he was surprised why did I not turn up for the important meeting. I conveyed the message to him that I am not feeling well and that I need to take a couple of days off. I got the message back that, he was concerned and wanted me to take rest, but wanted me back in the office quickly, as the time was to move fast on the department computerization project.

Finally, one day I called and Kalpana picked the phone and there was a strangeness in the atmosphere.

"Congratulations, I heard you are seeing someone," my voice was low.

There was a lull at the other end.

I repeated my question but this time with little anger.

"You had been avoiding me and I felt you did not want me anymore."

"You should have asked. I had told you that I am working hard for OUR future," I was very angry.

There was silence on the other end.

"Do you really know what has happened? I had a long discussion with your mother before leaving for Raymond. Because of her insistence and the promise, she took from me, I did not tell you anything and did not meet as often and kept working in a state of madness to prove my worth," and then I explained to her what has happened.

"How could I have known that and what else could I have done? It is too late now, I have moved on," she said in a low voice. And, I could sense the pain in that voice.

"So, now I am not any good for you, huh.....," I uttered in pain, disbelief, anger, and a feeling of dejection.

There was a lull for a few moments and then I disconnected.

"Fantastic, now when I was thinking that I was getting back on track, in my career and becoming materialistically successful, to an extent, I have been rejected and dumped even by the love of my life, my closest well-wisher," I ridiculed myself.

I just could not accept how fast things had changed, so I was still very furious. And in that desperation, I started stalking her. Waiting for hours outside her college and then follow her rickshaw on my bike. Many thoughts came to my mind like going to her home and shooting myself and her right in front of everyone and finishing the story.

I started wandering here and there senselessly on the bike. There is a place in Lucknow called 'Ups and Downs' in Arjunganj, where I was told the military gives training to their soldiers on riding motorbikes, in very difficult terrains. This is a very unique formation with climbs and slopes of various degrees and with sharp turns with sharp slips and with mud water in between. Very difficult terrain to ride a bike. I started riding my bike like crazy. I did not have any worry that, I may fall critically and either die or break my body parts. Many a time I used to get stuck in the mud and try to take out my bike desperately like I am trying to hurt Kalpana for what she has done to me. I kept calling her and trying to repeat the same thing, 'Why?'

One day she cried and pleaded to me "Please, let us move on," that was a very heavy day for me. I looked at myself in the mirror and asked "Who the hell are you? How can you harass and stalk the same person, you loved the most? This has to stop right now," I got a sense of guilt and promised not to bother her again.

I was hurt, felt like I was stabbed by the society once again. Brutally this time. If the M.Sc. debacle was rock bottom, then what is this?

I felt like I have been buried alive.

Chapter 11

"I am extremely sorry Boss for the last few days. I was not feeling well at all. But, I will try to make up for the lost time," I met my special secretary and made a humble submission to him.

"I hope you are fine now. Let us move fast because your story of pilot computerization has reached the principal secretary and he is very excited. He in turn has given some heads up to the chief secretary. So, we need to move real fast now," he explained the situation.

"Understood Boss. I will get on top of it immediately," I told him. I was still shattered but desperately wanted to immerse myself in work, so that I don't get any time to think.

In any state government structure, the senior-most IAS officer is the Chief Secretary who reports to the Chief Minister of the state. Our principal secretary reported to the chief secretary. Our Principal Secretary, Special Secretary, and Joint Secretary had portfolios of Technical Education, Non-Conventional Energy, and Civil Aviation. These were very important and critical portfolios and hence they used to be super busy. Such important and very senior IAS officers giving me importance was a very big thing for a youngster like me. I did not want to disappoint them any further and took the resolve to finish the work fast. I launched the pilot project and started monitoring it. The feedback and observations came and I corrected them quickly and made improvements. I had to showcase the project to our principal secretary. I planned an optimal presentation in the minimal time since senior bureaucrats do not have much time. I also planned to take feedback from the principal secretary to get the perspective of senior bureaucrats.

Despite being submerged in work, I still felt hurt thinking– Why me? How much more? Am I this bad? Is success so important? I did my self-retrospection to still understand what had just happened:

- "Probably, I got played by her mother. But she trusted me and felt cheated after she found about my affair with her daughter. Trust is one such delicate thing, once broken cannot be mended. Though, I had talked to her and made promises and even followed that, yet she may not have forgiven me. So, she did what any other parent would have done. She is not really at fault. She was just trying to protect her daughter. If I had got success in Engineering or M.Sc. then probably this may not have happened. My lack of success in society is the biggest reason for my rejection, once again. This thought made me further bitter.
- I felt that in the case of Kalpana, I was more at fault. I had told her that I am working hard for our future yet, I never told her the truth for being away due to the promises made to her mother. Unintentionally, but I may have pushed her away from me by talking more about studies rather than our love life. To prove my worth to society, I was indulging heavily in work which also may have disappointed her and taken her away from me. Maybe, her friends taunted her for me not being very successful, drifting her away from me. I was further disappointed and angry with this thought.

The more I thought, the more I was convinced that while it was circumstantial, yet the biggest reason is my being 'not very successful.'

"I have been thrashed, yet again, and this time to the bones, for not being materialistically successful. **Now**, I am not going to die, instead, I will put my entire might to ensure that I am materialistically successful. The rebel in me cried with tears of fire. My retaliation has picked the speed of a bullet train. I took admission in MBA in parallel to work and decided to slog to grow much faster.

The day of the presentation to the principal secretary came and I gave my presentation to him. He was very happy. But since he did not have much time, he quickly gave me thumbs up saying he will get the meeting fixed with Chief Secretary. Though, I did not get many inputs on my slides, I was happy that at least he was convinced and liked my overall presentation. I came back and started preparing for the chief secretary meeting with anxiety as this was a big thing for me.

"The demo has been fixed with the chief secretary next week," my special secretary, informed me.

"Sure Boss," I responded in a state of anxiety.

"But we need to prepare well because Chief Secretary has called Principal Secretary of all the departments," he announced.

"Oh, God. That is bad news. Will I be able to face all the top bureaucrats together?" I sounded nervous.

"Don't worry, prepare well and be confident. We will support you," he gave me confidence.

"Sure Boss, thanks," I thanked him.

I started preparing by revising my presentation and playing the storyline of my demo in my mind repeatedly. The final day came. We all gathered in the Chief Minister's Annex building where the Chief Secretary had his office. Our presentation was in a big central meeting hall with a big oval-shaped table behind which there were around 30 chairs in the front row.

Behind the first row of chairs, more chairs were kept in the second row. There was a big screen in the hall which was attached to the computer. I had called a person for assistance from IET, Lucknow to navigate the application. On one side of the round table, Chief Secretary was to sit, and on the opposite side, I was seated, and in between all the bureaucrats on both sides. We reached ahead of time in the meeting hall and prepared ourselves before the meeting. We were ready for the presentation and demo.

It was raining heavily outside with thunderstorms making the whole atmosphere a little more anxious. I thought a little rain is considered a good omen but was not sure what this thunderstorm meant. Just before the actual meeting time, my special secretary came and shared the news that our principal secretary is stuck with the Chief Minister out of the station and is not able to fly in the helicopter due to bad weather. I was disheartened and worried as I thought he will be a good person to save me in case something goes wrong. I realized that I am on my own now. I started gathering my courage.

Slowly, secretaries started coming into the meeting hall and then Chief Secretary also came in. And after initial greetings, we were given a go-ahead to start the presentation followed by the demo.

"Dear Sirs and Mams, I am here to present to you a pilot project in the form of a software application that has been developed to fine-tune, optimize and automate the functioning of a department section within the secretariat. We are presenting how this will work for a Model Section of Department of Technical Education," I started.

"Do you think you are going to change how a section works in the secretariat? It has been in place for a long time and is it possible to change the work process and the behavior of the people?" One of the senior secretaries interrupted me apprehensively.

I became very nervous but before I could say anything, to my surprise, the chief secretary interrupted him and asked him, "you do want the improvement of the section working, don't you? Let's hear him out." The tone was stern and impulsive as if telling him "You have to do it!"

The secretary nodded and became quiet. And that gave me an immediate feeling that I have the biggest supporter who seems to believe in this improvement initiative. With this confidence, I started my presentation and did not stop. I shared the current process, some case scenarios of the pain, expectation, and the need of the hour as well as the proposed improvement in the process. Then, I shared how all this will be automated with computerization to bring in efficiency and other benefits. The meeting lasted for around 45 minutes and it was over with the conclusion that "Chief Secretary has given a go-ahead to computerization of a model section in the technical education department and once this pilot will be successful then all the other departments will replicate this computerization process."

This was a HUGE SUCCESS for me. My first BIG project and presentation to such a large group of senior-most bureaucrats, was so smooth and successful. I sailed through without failure. My self-belief and confidence were immensely boosted and it further acted as fuel to my rebellion, retaliation, and the feeling of *Junoon*.

I CAN PROVE MY WORTH AND I WILL.

"Kalpana is getting engaged early next year," I got the news. Four months from now precisely. It felt like someone further sliced my broken heart. "I cannot stay in this city,", was my immediate reaction.

"Hi Boss, I need your valuable advice and support. I want to build a career in the USA, as soon as possible. Please help me understand what I need to do," I called PK and asked for his advice explaining my situation.

PK had moved to the headquarters of Raymond Woolen Mills located in Thane, Maharashtra. He had larger responsibility for creating a newer division of Raymond called the Raymond Consultancy Services (RCS). The idea was to support the IT of all the group companies and then start consultancy outside, to the rest of the world. He had established RCS and was running multiple transformation projects for group companies.

"My advice to you is that you will need to brush up your skills first for at least two years and then you can surely get many opportunities in the United States," he gave me his advice.

"Can you please help me with that?" I pleaded with my mentor.

"You can join me here in Thane. But then you will have to promise to stay with us for at least two years. Within that time, I can assure you that you will have appropriate skills which will help you to easily get opportunities in the USA," he offered me the solution and the deal.

"Fantastic. I assure you about two years in RCS and after that, I would explore opportunities in the USA for my further growth," I agreed.

"Good. Please share your updated resume and I will help you with the offer letter. When do you want to join?" He further asked.

"I surely want to join by end of February 1995," I gave him a firm reply.

I knew very well what I needed to do now. I went back home and told my decision about my parents. Both were taken aback, as they could see my success and growth here, and just a few days back, I had shared with them, my success story in the secretariat and the approval of the chief secretary on my project. They were not expecting this at all. But, I told them very clearly that this is my final decision and I am not going to change it at any cost. My mother understood my firmness as she knew about my breakup and hurt, so she did not confront me. My father was very disheartened and tried to talk about this, but unsuccessfully. I was hard as a rock. I was on a mission.

"Boss, this is my resignation. I want to move back to the private sector as I want to learn and move abroad," I told the joint secretary politely but firmly. He was shocked. I had given him a hint earlier about my breakup and resolve to prove quickly in the private sector and maybe in the USA.

"But what about the computerization of the model section of technical education, that you have worked on so hard? And remember, Chief Secretary has already approved it," he was a little perplexed.

"Boss, I promise that I will do as much as I can before going. There was a programmer, I had loaned from IET earlier, I can bring him to speed up the project. Besides, please let me know who can replace me and I will transition my learning to that person as well. Anyways, the bigger part of conceptualization, design, development, testing, and pilot is already done. So, it will not be that difficult. I have worked so hard on this project, so, I would want to see this getting implemented successfully," I tried to give him confidence.

"But this is all your work and you must cross the last mile and take credit," he still insisted.

"Boss, you know my condition, I will not survive if I stay back here. I am not hungry for credit; I never was. But the most important thing in my life for me, right now, is to get on the right path of exponential growth, which only the private sector can give, and by getting an opportunity abroad," I pleaded with him to accept my resignation.

"Even if I agree, Special Secretary will not let you go," he spoke.

"I will request him as well," I told him.

I met Special Secretary and told him about my decision and plans. He already had got the news from my father as my father played well by reaching to him and asking him to convince me to stay back. "Wow dad, what a move. But I have taken the final decision that cannot be changed." I was talking in my head.

"Why are you so stubborn and want to go after all this fantastic work," he seemed irritated.

"Ok Boss, now you have to listen to my brief story and the reason behind it," and then I gave him a little glimpse of my reasons.

He was a little surprised but then he touched my shoulder and said, "**Here is my advice and offer to you.** Take a two-year sabbatical leave and I will give that to you as an exception. Go and try it out as you did in BEC-Jhansi and if you want to come back after that at least you will not lose your well-deserved government job with well-established credibility. But if you will resign and go, then coming back will not be possible," he offered a fantastic deal with a lot of consideration.

My eyes got moist and my heart filled with gratitude with his such an unusual consideration. "Boss. Please understand that I have been in a government job for the last four years and you know, I have put my heart and soul into my work,

I even have gone out of my expected work area to try to give more and achieve more. But honestly, this work is still not at the expected levels of the private sector, which means, I lag in terms of knowledge than what my colleagues have got in the last four years in the private sector. This essentially means going back, at this stage of my career, I will struggle to gain the expected level of knowledge. And this will surely mean that I may get into moments of weaknesses and frustration there. And if at that time, I will have an easy carrot of government job hanging, as per your offer, then there is a possibility that I may not try enough in the private sector and will come back. And that will not be right for my resolve. Hence, I think it will be best for me to resign and go with no return option so that I have no option but to succeed," I told him genuinely.

He laughed and said "You are one of a kind. Firstly, people don't get such offers that I am giving you, and secondly, those who rarely get it never leave such offer."

I kept quiet with my head hung a little.

"Ok, if that is what you want, I will not stop you. All the very best. But plan the handover so your work here does not get impacted negatively," he agreed.

"Absolutely Boss. I have already talked to the Joint secretary and it is in my interest to make it successful. I have conceptualized this and put my heart and soul. I will also do whatever is needed," I assured him.

The Rebel in me was all set
for the Retaliation with Resolve.

Chapter 12

My best friend, Vivek, was getting engaged and I was delighted. Though, I had met him for the first time, only a decade back, yet he had become an integral part of my life. I met him first time when he became my neighbor in Kaisarbagh Officer's Colony in Lucknow. He did his B.Tech. from IET, Lucknow, and then did his M.Tech. from IIT Delhi. He subsequently qualified for Indian Engineering Services and was selected in Indian Ordnance Factory Services. When I joined Raymond Cements, he joined the Indian Ordnance Factory at Jabalpur. No matter where we lived thereafter, we used to be in constant touch either through long letters, phone calls, or visiting. We have been like real brothers.

Even in my state of sorrow, I was very happy for his engagement. Both our families and relatives knew about our amazing friendship. I created a very unique memory album, of rare photos of Vivek, with a storyline, and presented it to his fiancé, Pratima. I thought that was a wonderful personalized precious gift. And she loved it too.

Vivek is a very sincere and practical person. When my M.Sc. Physics debacle happened and I was shattered, he was the one who gave me hard-hitting advice, to prove my worth to society and encouraged me that I can do it. Vivek also knew about my relationship with Kalpana. He tried to console me but I was in a different frame of mind.

I had told my mother, about my breakup as well. And she was very concerned seeing me and my state of mind. She tried to help me come out of it but was not successful. The continuous shocks on the curves of my life, in recent years, had made me, heartbroken, rebellious, negative but at the same time,

I became very determined to retaliate and prove my worth. This resulted in me being, very myopic and biased and I was unable to appreciate the other good things around me. My mother became very worried about this change in my nature and my rebellious behavior. When I resigned from my current job at World Bank and Technical Education Department, and accepted an offer from the Raymond Consultancy Services (RCS), she became further worried, that I will be alone far away from home, in this mental state. Mostly, she was worried that I should not end up hurting myself.

Vivek got engaged and his marriage was scheduled around mid-February 1995. Accordingly, I had planned my joining in RCS, a week after Vivek's marriage, by end of February. We both had only a couple of months left for our next important milestones. My mother was becoming very restless and insisted that I should at least get engaged before leaving for Thane, but I was clear that I don't want to marry.

My mother called Vivek and they both conspired and created a strategy to emotionally blackmail and convince me for the marriage. They both insisted that "Marriage is a very important institution that everyone must follow. You may not feel the urge right now, but after a while, you will feel lonely in life, as other family and friends will start their own married life, and become busier with their own families. In that scenario, you will not fit in, as your priorities and expectations will be much different than that of your friends. And that will hurt you, and make you feel lonely, and by that time it will be very difficult for you to turn around your decision." Then, as usual, Vivek played his card, giving me the hard practical advice. "You are fighting against the society, so even if you succeed materialistically, you will still not be considered a normal person if you are not married."

The ADVICE and arguments made sense, though I didn't like them.

Finally, after a lot of arguments, I gave up and agreed. My thought was that, if I marry then I need to do justice with the girl I marry, as I did not want to spoil an innocent life. I promised myself that I will give my 100% to this relationship. My mother wanted me to marry before I leave to join RCS in Thane, but then we agreed that I will get engaged before leaving for Thane and marry within a year.

In those times there were no matchmaking websites, like shaadi.com. Arranged marriages were fixed either through reference, network, or an advertisement in the newspaper. We started looking for all the routes. We gave an advertisement in *Times of India* newspaper. The responses use to come in a PO Box in the *Times of India* building. After around a week of advertisement, when I first visited the TOI building to bring back the responses, there were around 40 responses. As they say, "Your match is already made in heaven," when I was looking at the pictures and biodata of the proposals, my eyes got fixed to the Anita's picture and I thought "She is the one."

As a part of the formal matchmaking process, we responded to the proposal, and Anita's family came to our house to meet us and discuss the marriage proposal. Since, I already had liked her picture , the rest of the discussions were only a formality from our side. As a typical next step, it was decided that the boy and girl should formally meet along with the families. As an auspicious place, it was decided that the families will meet in a small park within the campus of the famous Bhootnath temple, in Indira Nagar, Lucknow.

Anita wore a cream color saree. When I looked at her face, her eyes somehow seemed very familiar to me, and I got the same feeling again "She is the one." As, I had seen in the picture, she indeed was very lean and petite. With so many people around, we did not get the opportunity to talk to each other alone, besides a few pleasantries.

I gave my consent later that day, as I had felt some kind of connection with her. But, I wanted to talk to her alone, before the marriage, as I wanted to share my critical past, and then know her response. Our meeting was arranged and I took Anita to Neebu Park (one of the newly developed parks near the famous Bara Imambara in Lucknow.) We sat down in a corner and I started the conversation:

"I want to tell you about some of the critical things of my past which I think you should know before you give your response," I told her.

She nodded and kept listening with a serious face.

"I had a serious relationship in the past. But now that it is broken, it is my past. I promise, not to bring my past in my marriage," I revealed.

She heard and then said, "That's fine, but I have a question for you."

"Please ask," I was curious.

"Do you smoke?" She asked innocently.

I smiled at her innocent question and replied "I do not smoke. I always have wondered why people smoke and I think when people link it with some of their emotions like happiness, sadness, anxiety, or relaxation, then they get hooked to it. It is a psychological thing in my opinion. With the understanding of this logic, when I was in class 12th, I had decided, that I will try to taste a cigarette in normal situations, to see how is the taste and impact. One day, I along with my close friends, decided to take one puff each of at least 10 different brands to see the impact. But, I did not find anything extraordinary to get hooked to, rather we did not like the taste at all.

So, we concluded that our theory is right that smoking addiction is linked to one's own psychological emotion. Since then, I have not smoked." I gave her the complete background of my smoking venture and why I do not smoke. Anita was happy with my response. We both agreed to the marriage.

Vivek's marriage was scheduled for 18th February. We decided to keep my engagement on 22nd February so that both of us can attend each other's functions. I decided to join RCS on 25th February.

It was very rejuvenating to see Vivek getting married. Finally, the day came and I got engaged and promised myself that I will give my best to Anita and will not let my past relationship impact our marriage.

I was still very upset with the materialistic world and the criteria of society in defining who is a good or bad, successful or unsuccessful person. "What an irony!" That's why I resolved, that I will live within the society and will ensure that I am not considered a failure and will not allow anyone to criticize me.

The Rebel in me was all set to start 'Intensified Retaliation'. Thane-Mumbai was the next Karma-Kshetra.

Chapter 13

Mumbai Meri Jaan

"He is Sudeep Verma," PK introduced me to the team at Raymond Consultancy Services (RCS) and gave me my background after I reached Thane and joined RCS. It was so heartening to see a team of young energetic professionals who were going to be my colleagues. The atmosphere was very energetic.

RCS was located in Thane (twin city of Mumbai) and was a brainchild of PK. He had convinced Singhania's to start an IT consulting services company, which will serve customers globally, like any other Information Technology Services company.

The IT sector was going through a huge surge and profitability. And with further liberalization of early 1991, there was a huge demand for computerization, automation, resourcing from within India and outside the world. Hence the demand for IT professionals was further growing day by day. Everyone wanted to take advantage of this opportunity. Business houses started investing in IT companies to grow a profitable business. Talent forces from all engineering streams started targeting IT industry jobs, as there was good money, growth, and an opportunity to go to the western world, primarily to the USA.

While leaders at Raymond's decided to invest in the IT consultancy division, they gave an initial target to complete computer transformation, within the Raymond group companies like Raymond Woolen, Raymond Cement, Park Avenue, Raymond Steel, Singhania Hospital, etc. There were 13 diversified group companies within the Raymond organization. PK had targeted to complete internal organizational transformation within 2-3 years, after which the focus would move to external companies. At the time of my joining RCS, multiple such internal transformation projects were in progress.

During my induction, I started learning the latest technologies of SYBASE and Power Builder. In the meanwhile, I was also told to start understanding the processes of some of the transformation initiatives as well. I had no distractions and started my task immediately.

I also had requested the University to transfer my MBA study center to a nearby location in Mumbai, so that I can continue my focus on MBA as well. I was allocated to a study center located in Mulund which was close to Thane but came under Mumbai city. I had opted for the classes over the weekend, and with my motorbike with me, it was easy for me to commute. I was all set to work hard during the day and study hard during the nights and the weekends.

I had mingled with the team very well, quickly, as they were mostly of my age or younger. This was my first interaction with the Mumbai-folks and they were very energetic and fun-loving people. We used to work very hard. In the evening, we had get togethers. Beer was a very regular evening culture and, I observed most of the young female colleagues used to drink beer. I loved the broad-minded thinking of people around there. I felt connected, aligned, and at home.

"You need to go and help the IFAS project team as they are facing problems," PK asked me. IFAS was the Integrated Financial Account System project to transform the Finance department of the flagship company, Raymond Woolen Works, from its old legacy applications provided by third-party vendors based on Cobol, to developing in-house applications on the latest technologies of Sybase and Power Builder. The project was running late from the planned schedule. The project was to go Live on 1st April 1995, but was running severely behind schedule. Originally, I was to be deployed in other projects, but due to the delays in the most critical project, PK had asked me to temporarily help the IFAS project team. This was critical because Raymond had not renewed the services contract of the legacy application. This means if the IFAS project is not live by 1st April then Raymond Woolen will be in deep trouble for not having validated finance books (ledgers, journals, trial balance, and GLs). It was a mission-critical project for the flagship company of the group.

I went to the Raymond Woolen office building which was next to the Raymond Woolen factory. This was within a big Raymond premise, in which many group companies were located like Raymond, Woolens, Raymond Steel, JK Files, Park Avenue, Raymond Consultancy, etc. I told PK that I have never worked on any financial accounting application so, I have zero knowledge of the domain processes and applications. He assured me that I will get the required help. I accepted the challenge. I met the project manager, who asked for help on the 'Reconciliation' system, which was a subsystem of the overall IFAS application. I was assigned one person with me to finish the program faster. We worked day and night to complete the program. In this whole duration, the project team of the IFAS project was working on the overall project.

One morning, I reached the office and saw that the large team of the overall project, has not reached the office. Within a few hours, the news spread that the large team has quit and joined another company through which they are going to the USA. This came as a shock and a huge crisis moment for the company. By late night the news was confirmed that the team including all the key senior members have left the company without much information and handover.

By the mid-1990s the demand for Indian IT software professionals grew tremendously in the USA, and many Indian companies used to poach good professionals, get their work visa done and then send them either directly through their company or in a body-shopping mode. Body-shopping was a very commonly used term at that time. In body-shopping, a company that needs a software professional (resource), used to contact placement agencies in India who used to send the required resources at an hourly or daily rate. One such big company, working from Pune, was sending software professionals (resources) to the USA, very frequently and in large numbers. And we were told that this company had poached the major IFAS team members and sent them to the USA. Though it was a big shock, on the other hand, it was good to see job opportunities in the USA.

The next day, PK along with other senior persons, started assessing the damage. One senior assessed that not much of the work has been done, and there is no way the new IFAS application can be made live on 1st April. This meant a huge crisis since the legacy application was to stop on 31st March. Financial account being the backbone, the company will be drastically impacted. This indeed was a grave situation. On the next day, many senior-level meetings happened in Raymond Woolen, along with all other key persons, like auditors to try to salvage the alarming situation. I could see PK, Finance Head, and other senior professionals having long meetings and discussions.

"Sudeep, the situation is very alarming. I am asking you to take over the project," PK explained the situation after the meeting and told me.

"As mentioned earlier, I have no idea of Financial Account," I replied.

Chapter 14

"But Boss, there are multiple factors that make me very uncomfortable. Firstly, I have no idea of Financial Accounting, secondly, the timelines are just impossible, thirdly, this is a very high-stake project at which I cannot fail," I shared my apprehension.

"I will assign senior-most people who can help you on the financial accounting domain and processes, so you don't have to worry about that. As far as timeline is concerned, we have managed time till June which means you have around 3.5 months. On your last point of visibility, I will be there, along with the head of the finance department, to manage that," he tried to give me comfort.

"What if I fail, and I see great chances of that," I shared my worry.

"You just give your best and forget about the rest. I am assuring you that nobody will blame you or the team. I will manage that. The team that flew has done the damage and you are just giving your best to try to resolve the critical situation," he gave me further comfort.

"What about the team? There is no one from the old-team and it seems there is not much of documentation either," I was inquisitive.

"We will create a new team along with you. I will also ask Martin to help you since he was involved in the application design process. Additionally, there are a couple of the old team members who can be helpful," he was trying to create the best support system.

"Who will help us with financial accounting processes?" I was eager.

"Let us go to the finance department tomorrow, after the team formation, and I will talk to the finance head and will try to get you the best possible help," he decided.

"Ok Boss as you say. I trust you completely, so I will give my best shot," I agreed.

"My advice to you is to give your best and do not get worried about the outcome. All I can tell you is that there will be tremendous learning in this project, and you will only gain from it. **Tough situations give the best learnings," he gave me another invaluable Advice.** I felt comfortable with all the support he was offering besides his assurance to manage senior stakeholders.

The next day the team was formed. I did not know much of the background of many people, so I left it to PK to help me with that, as I trusted his judgment. The senior manager who was involved in the initial designing of the IFAS application was told to help us in understanding the design of the application. A core team of 8 members was formed, and I was assured to get the support of additional resources if needed. Out of this eight-member team, three team members were those who were part of the original project team and the rest five, including me, were new to the project. Key team members were Mukund, Rohini, Sapna, Parveen, Mani, Pravin, and Jai besides me. Unfortunately, all of the senior team members from the original project team had left the organization, so we were not aware of the flow of the programs/ application and design.

The following day, PK took us to the finance department, and we had a meeting with the head of the finance department along with the division heads under him like payable head, receivable head, etc. The meeting started with a very intense mode, with everybody highly concerned due to the critical situation.

"We have allocated the new project team, and the team will work in a mission mode to finish the project by the new defined timeline of end of June. Sudeep will lead the project. We will need support from everyone from the finance department side, to help this team to complete the task on priority," PK informed and asked for complete support from the finance team.

"This is the topmost priority for all of us, so you will get complete support from all of us. Please be rest assured," the Finance head replied and all other heads also assured their full support.

"What kind of support are you expecting from our side?" The finance head asked curiously.

"To start with, I am expecting two types of support. First, I want senior persons from all finance divisions, who can help us any time, if we have any questions regarding any processes, like payable, receivable, journals, ledgers, etc. Secondly, we may also need help from individual divisions on the data and its validation. So, it will be good to identify such team members and allocate them to us," I explained.

"We are going to work on this project in a war mode, we will need additional support from all the seniors as well. Since, we will work in a 24X7 type of schedule, we will not know when we will face an issue, so will require persons to be available to resolve the issue as and when we need it," I continued.

"Sure, that makes sense. We will work out the support structure and then discuss it with you. But be assured that you will get all the possible help from our side," the finance head assured.

"I will be there to personally support you guys as and when you need any help," the head of receivable, assured.

"Same here. Once again, this is the topmost priority for all of us," the payable head also assured. All other seniors too reiterated support.

"Thank you so much for your assurances, we will never be successful without your support and without working as ONE TEAM," I thanked everyone for the support shown.

We started the work. First, we assessed the current situation. The design, was quite complex, and to understand it. Then we started assessing the current situation of the development work to understand and estimate the pending work and create a concrete revised project plan. This was a problem, as there was no one to hand over the actual development work. Hence, we started reverse engineering, to see the programs and then try to correlate the same with the design. This was a more time taking process but we had no other option. I took sessions from the finance department seniors on the accounting process, and then understood the complexities of finance processes. We took a lot of help to understand the process.

We were working in a war mode, spending 24X7 time in the office. There were times when we used to sleep in the server room, spreading large 132 column printer papers on the floor. We were so deeply involved, in the project and its processes, that we even used to see the programs in our dreams. And to my utter surprise, for the first time in my life, I did get an answer to a problem that I was not able to solve during the day. So intense was our involvement.

Many times, we missed our lunch, forgetting the time of the day and the canteen timings. This news reached PK and the finance head, and they arranged our food in the guest house nearby, in case we miss our meal and felt hungry. To our delight, we were told that we can also get beers in the guest house. This was to relax and break the fatigue.

Our team constitution was that of mostly very young and single persons, and that had a benefit that they were focused and dedicated to the project, without any pressure from home. But being young has another side as well. There was love, affairs, flirting all around. Luckily, I was engaged, so I was not distracted. I was the project manager but acted more like a friend to the team, so I knew all that was going around. Some of the team members getting tired at 2 AM used to call their GFs/BFs and they used to have long talks. I never discouraged this as this used to work as rejuvenation for the team members.

Around the end of May, we got hold of the overall project and knew exactly how much work was left. Now that only one month was left, the pressure and anxiety were building more and more day by day. By June-mid, we had very mixed feelings, as we were happy to see that we were getting close to the completion of the work, yet, the time pressure was making us nervous. We asked the finance team to start entry of the April to June (till date) in the system. A week before going live, we decided to print vouchers for the first week of April so that we can be sure of the right entries. We printed and faced some issues, so the next morning we brought the finance team, to find out the root causes. We found two root causes and fixed them by the evening.

Five days to Go Live, THAT NIGHT was the moment of truth for us.

Chapter 15

We all had not shaved for months, and most of us used to look like absent-minded professors, and not the smart IT professionals. Nobody cared about what dresses we were wearing and how we looked.

More than three months of continuous 24X7 working had started taking a toll on our bodies. However, the time pressure was such that we did not even realize our fatigue, pressure on the body, and lack of sleep. The only thing on our mind was that we have to ensure that project goes Live on 1st July. Till now, no one was putting any pressure on us directly, but we all could see the pressure, on the faces of all the group heads. In between, we used to see, the auditors also having meetings with the senior officials from the finance department. While no one was saying anything about the timeline, yet we all could feel the pressure in the atmosphere. That made us a little nervous as well.

After understanding the two root causes, we fixed the programs.

"This is the moment of truth for all of us," I addressed the team.

"We have worked very hard and we are almost there," I continued.

"Once all the vouchers are tallied then we know we have won the major battle, then we can proceed to complete for the rest of the books like journals and ledgers, as all programs are ready," I added.

"Conversion programs have been run to put the data from 1st April till date, so we can print all the vouchers. Let us print the vouchers for April month and tally them," I shared the plan of action.

"All the best folks, may God bless us all," I finished my address, and we all proceeded for our respective tasks.

We started printing the vouchers for April month. We had two finance department team members, to support us if we needed any help.

After some time, when all the vouchers for April got printed, we took the printout and went to the conference room.

We looked at the very first voucher and it was completely wrong.

"What the hell!" We exclaimed in a state of shock.

"But this voucher was right till yesterday?" I asked in a state of shock.

A day before, when we took help from the finance team, we were working on exceptional and complicated vouchers and had found the root cause for that.

"Let us evaluate all the vouchers quickly, and see how many vouchers are wrong, and what kind of pattern of the issue is seen," I tried to control my emotions and look at the complete picture before reacting.

As the teams started looking at the vouchers, we started seeing that many vouchers were wrong and not matching.

WE WERE IN A STATE OF HUGE SHOCK.

We all sat back and for a few minutes, nobody spoke. Our faces were blank. For a minute, I thought we have lost the battle. Being the leader, it was my responsibility, for the success of the project and team. I decided to look into the programs. I tried to take corrective action, instead of giving up. But were not able to pinpoint the issue.

The complete team was exhausted. Due to the time pressure and steep targets, we had not focused on our exhaustion, fatigue, and tiredness. We all were having high hopes of crossing the first major milestone tonight, but when the vouchers failed, our hopes started falling like a pack of cards and our mental and physical fatigue took over us, and our morale started falling vertically.

We did not have enough time, and this felt like the end of the road.

The news went to the other team members and they also came and we all felt like we have lost the battle. For some time, we just sat there, without anyone speaking anything, with our heads hung down.

"What shall we do now?" One of the team members asked.

There was silence in the room. I said "Let us take a walk outside."

We all got up and started walking out of the accounts department and out of the Raymond Woolen building, to the main gate.

Inside the big premise of the Raymond, there was a Hanuman temple close to the main gate. We reached the temple in complete silence. It was around 2 AM in the night. The temple was closed, but we sat on the temple boundary wall. The hard work of the last 3.5 months, had emotionally attached us to the project. The disaster today had left all of us emotionally devastated. While this project was very critical for the organization, yet on the personal front, this was a question of 'Do or Die' for me, as I was desperately looking for success to grow and establish myself. After the government job, this was my first assignment and I did not want to be tagged a failure. The success of this project would have given me much-needed confidence and the right path that I was looking for myself.

"Why is this happening to me yet again?" I thought.

"What have I done wrong? How much are you going to test me?" I thought, looking at the Hanuman temple and the sky with moist eyes.

I saw some other team members also had tears in their eyes.

"What shall we do?" whispered one team member.

It was like someone shrugged me in the morning and said "Wake up."

Different thoughts started pouring in from different team members.

"We gave the best we could have, but unfortunately we did not have enough time. What else we could have done?"

"Can we ask for more time? But we have been told that it is critical to have books in place at the end of the quarter."

"We all also can leave without any notice as the original team did."

"But what will people say, if we just abscond without information?"

"No matter what seniors say, but on the ground, the finance team has high hopes from us, and they will feel so disappointed with us."

"How can we face them?"

"What will PK say, if we just disappear?"

I was further terrified at the idea of just absconding, but I was also in the giving-up mode. I told the team, "Let us call Sharma Ji, and tell him the project status, and then we will take a final call on our next move". Sharma Ji was 2nd in command to PK and had been supporting us on this project. Though, it was 2 AM, since everyone knew that we work in 24X7 mode, hence we had the liberty to call him. We sent a message to Sharma Ji, "This is an emergency, please meet us outside temple." We waited for some time and then saw Sharma Ji coming.

"What happened?" he asked seeing our miserable body language.

"We had fixed the identified root causes and then printed the vouchers for April. When we checked, we found most of them are wrong and are not matching," I explained to him.

"But how come most of the vouchers be wrong?" he was surprised.

"We have looked at the program but do not have any clue," I replied.

"It seems, I have failed everyone," I was disappointed and choking.

"We all are feeling like running away from here. But we don't think it is right to go without informing. That is why we called you. I have no idea how to inform PK about this," I shared our mental status.

He heard us for a moment and then said.

"You all still have 4 more days to go for the Go Live," He spoke.

"**My ADVICE** to you is to keep trying for the next 4 days that you have in hand. You already have spent the last 3.5 months working 24X7 putting your heart and soul, so continuing for another 4 days shall not be a problem. In all probability, and as per my experience, there may be a simple mistake which you may be able to resolve if you work with a fresh mind. If at all, after working for the remaining 4 days also, you are not able to fix the issues, you can still decide to go and I will not stop you. But you shall not give up without fighting till the last day. If you go now, anyways you will keep on thinking about this as a failure for life, but if you fight till the end, you will either succeed or will have the satisfaction that you gave your best till the end," he concluded.

We all looked at each other and found this advice making much sense. With such hard work, none of us wanted to give up, but with the failure of vouchers, our emotions got on top of us and we felt weak.

We decided to call it a day and to resume working with a fresh mind. We felt a little relaxed after the advice and went to sleep.

Chapter 16

We reached the office after sleep. After the night's discussion, we wanted to give our 100%, with renewed energy to resolve the issue.

"I need your help and guidance," I asked receivable, payable heads.

"Sure, how can we help," they both asked.

"It looks like there is some minor logic issue which is making some vouchers wrong. I want to take a few original vouchers depicting different scenarios and walk through the programs to see where have we gone wrong in our logic," I explained the problem to them.

"Sure, let us get to it immediately," they said and we sat in the room.

We started with the first voucher and step by step looking at the program to see what should be the figures in different accounts at each stage. To our surprise and delight, the very first problem was identified in a formula where there was a gap of addition and deletion. In that formula, while fixing the problem a day back, the debit was taken as a deduction from the account of the debtor, and credit was taken as an addition to the account of the debtor. This was exactly the opposite, for the given scenario, and while fixing one of the formulae by mistake the correct formula was also changed. We felt so happy yet stupid. We looked for the logic for various other types of vouchers and found only one more similar mistake in one of the exceptional cases. Rest all vouchers, that we looked at, seemed fine from the logical perspective. We were happily anxious now.

We started printing only the identified vouchers that we had just validated to see the outcome.

"All the vouchers are absolutely fine," shouted the team member.

There was an immediate wave of happiness among all of us. With a little more effort, we found the rest of the issues as well. After fixing that bug, we again printed the vouchers and validated them. To our delight, all of them got tallied. We were inside the server room and, with this validation, we all shouted in happiness. The shout was so loud that all the people from nearby cabins and cubicles came to see what was happening. We informed that all April vouchers are tallied correctly. There was a roar of cheers from the finance team.

"Let us now print all the vouchers from 1st May till yesterday, and tally them to see, if at all, there is any other problem left, either that of data issue or exceptional handling," I told the team, and we all started working on that. The team printed all the vouchers from May till the current date and started tallying date by date. Barring a few the rest were tallying. We analyzed, identified, and fixed them as well.

All the vouchers were now tallied. This was a big relief as we knew that one of the most important problems is now resolved. We had spent only around two hours and all the vouchers had been corrected.

The project team gathered in the server room, and we all looked at each other. Just a few hours back, in the night, we were thinking of giving up and running away. And merely two hours of effort, with a fresh and positive frame of mind, has changed the situation completely in our favor. From the gloom to the glory.

Learning: "Often the gap from failure to success is minuscule. Only those who try till the end, can find that.

Perseverance with patience and positivity is the key," *we had just realized that.*

The team had tasted the first big success and was full of confidence and zeal. They had started getting a sense of achievement. We started working on the rest of the planned tasks.

Next in line was the journals, and besides some minor problems, primarily related to the data issues, we did not find any problem in the journals. We fixed the same and printed all the journals again and found them to be correct. Now, we needed ledgers to be correct.

Two days before the Go Live date, we converted the data of the previous night and printed the general ledger (GL). We did find a few problems in the GL. With the experience of not rushing into the feeling of negativity in the hour of pressure, we looked at all the problems with a calm mind and analyzed them. We quickly identified and resolved all of the issues and found that the GL is getting tallied and is in a good shape. We decided not to share this success yet, with either the finance team or the RCS leaders. But, to reduce their anxiety, we did indicate to them, that things are looking fine so far. We decided to let the finance team finalize the June data so that the quarter ending is done, after which we will convert the final data of the quarter and print the final books of the quarter.

We were informed the next day, that the June data has been closed, and the quarter data is also finalized by the finance teams.

"Let us have early dinner today and start acting on the quarterly books," I told the team. We finished the dinner by 9 PM and came back to our working space on the finance department floor.

All the data was tallied and the books except GL were printed and tallied. We were super excited as we could see the success right in front of us. All the data entry screens were already tested correctly.

We started printing General Ledgers for all three months. We started printing the same around 3 AM and printed all of them by 4 AM. We looked at the GL closely and found them to be completely in order.

IS THIS IT? We were still not able to believe it. We were all super excited. There was a sense of enormous achievement, a feeling of pride, for completing the humongous project in time. Taking an almost impossible project with unimaginable timelines and still completing that successfully, within given timelines, instilled huge confidence and self-belief in me, that "I can do anything."

When one gets confidence, one becomes bold. I was having that feeling. I felt like having fun and trying to surprise the senior leaders.

"Let us print three sets of GLs for April, May, and June and put first set on the desk of Finance Head in his cabin, the second set in PK's cabin, and the third one in the server room for our reference later," I asked the team, and they happily executed that.

"Let us write a cover page with the caption, '*GL from April to June. With Complements from the IFAS Project Team. Please validate,*' and place the same in the room of finance head and PK," I shared the plan.

By the time we had placed the complete printed GL, on their desks, it was around early morning time.

"Let us now get out of this place to treat ourselves with a nice breakfast outside and from there let us go to watch the morning movie show," I suggested and gave a wink to the team.

"This is a fantastic idea," the team was excited, originally with a sense of achievement and fulfillment, and now with a sense of naughtiness.

We packed our stuff and left the premises before the regular work hour started. I carried my 'Pager device' just for precaution.

In those times there were no mobile phones and instead, there was a new technology called 'Pager' that had just started. A 'Pager' is a small telecommunications device that receives (and, in some cases, transmits) alert signals and/or short messages. This type of device is convenient for people expecting telephone calls, but who are not near a landline telephone set to make or return calls immediately. The simplest one-way pagers display the return-call telephone number of the person who sent the message.

We went to a restaurant and treated ourselves to a good breakfast. Then we went to watch a morning movie show. I could see some messages and phone numbers on my pager. But, I smiled and purposefully ignored them. I knew by now there must be a huge stir in the office. But I was sure, that the nature of the stir must be positive, however, they must be perplexed about the overall status.

"Nothing to worry about. We had so many days and nights of restlessness, during the project cycle, so, they can taste a little restlessness too," I thought mischievously. We decided to go for a 12–3 PM show as well. We were on roll. We thoroughly enjoyed it. In between, I kept receiving texts on my pager but did not respond.

Finally, we reached Raymond premises, around 4 PM. Some people saw us coming at the main gate. By the time we reached the finance floor, there were many people including the seniors waiting for us. They saw smiles on our faces and understood the situation.

"We had printed all the books in the night and thought it will take time for you to validate so we went out to take a break," I smiled.

"Books are all looking good and tallied. Is there anything else that is left or we are good to Go Live?" many leaders asked at the same time.

"From our side, we think everything is done for the go-live. So, we are Live now as per our understanding," I confirmed my understanding. There was a huge cheer across the floor.

PK also arrived and asked the same question with a smile, "All done?"

"Yes, all planned tasks are completed. We are LIVE now," I replied.

"Fantastic job everyone!" PK was overwhelmed. He always had been a man of few but thoughtful words.

Multiple celebrations took place in the coming days. Our work was recognized everywhere. From our perspective, we all had a sense of achievement, satisfaction, fulfillment, and **enormous confidence**. The biggest realization was:

- Perseverance and Patience brings Positive results.
- One can do anything, if, one puts his/her heart and soul into it.
- One shall not give up till the last moment.
- ***Often the gap from failure to success is minuscule.***
- A fresh mind gives better results than a fatiguing one.
- Always seek advice to check if you are not clogged with bias.
- The brightest view comes after the darkest tunnel.

Chapter 17

I had not spoken with my fiancé, Anita, for quite a few days now. I had told her earlier about the project crisis, and how we were working in a 24X7 mode, so calling was not possible.

In the 1990s, there were no mobile phones, and landline phones were the only mode of communication besides letters. Since, there were only a few dedicated STD phone lines in the office, hence it was difficult to make frequent long-distance calls, from the office. The only option, for me, was to call her in Lucknow, from an STD Booth. In the late 1990s, STD booths were very popular for telecommunication, but the STD call rates were very high. To give some relief, the call rates used to go down significantly after 9 PM. As a result, there used to be a long queue after 9 PM at the STD booths. Adding to the complexity and misery of communication, there was no phone in Anita's house, at that time. The only way to call her was to make a call at the house of Anita's fast friends Sonica and Monica, who lived six houses away from Anita's house. With this complexity, the sequence of calls to Anita was like this:

1. First go to the STD booth and get in a queue just before 9 PM.
2. On my turn, after 9 PM, I used to call her friend and request her to call Anita saying that I will call back after 15-20 minutes.
3. Then, I used to get to the back of the queue once again.
4. Her friend used to go and call Anita while, I used to be in the queue.

5. My next number to call back, used to come depending on how many people are in the queue and how long they talk.
6. I used to call back again once my number comes into the queue.
7. By this time, Anita used to be at her friend's home.
8. During my call to Anita, two interesting factors were there:
    a. People around me were eager for their turn, waiting for me to complete my call, and used to listen to my conversation.
    b. Anita used to talk with people around in the room listening.

This was the only way we could talk, during our courtship period. In current times, people may not even realize that feeling we got from that type of call. But even that call used to give us a good feeling. I guess when you have limited means, then you realize your importance.

I shared with Anita, my success and, the feeling of achievement. I told her, "now my path seems to be very clear. I will continue my hard work so that I can continue to grow much faster and ultimately go to the USA to achieve the pinnacle of success that I have planned." She heard and supported me. We had our romantic discussions and the plan for the marriage. We felt emotional, and I decided to visit Lucknow for a couple of days after my MBA exams.

I had put my full focus on MBA papers and thought that this is the right time for me to attempt more papers, quickly. To complete my MBA, I needed to clear 19 papers and a final project report submission. I had already cleared 5 papers and was still left with 14 papers and a project report. I analyzed that

I need to complete, remaining papers and project, in around 18 months. I went to the study center and planned my course schedule. I smiled at my stars and started preparing for MBA exams at a war level. My weekday schedule continued to be of 18 hours with around 12 hours in the office and 4 hours of studies and 2 hours of relaxation and fun with friends. I was sleeping for only 5 hours a day. During weekends, my focus was primarily on studies and some time for fun with friends.

Post-Go-live project work was going on as per plan. The news of the IFAS project Go-live spread fast and other divisions like Raymond Limited-Kenya, J.K. (Bombay) Limited, Raymond Steel, J.K. Engineering & Files, SSSH Medical Research Center, Thane, also started putting pressure on their projects. But, I was seeing more opportunities within Raymond Woolen to automate other peripheral systems and integrate them with IFAS. The success of IFAS increased the demand of businesses for more automation. I wanted to take things at work a little slow, for the next month and a half, due to my MBA papers. I decided to take larger projects post my exams and Lucknow visit.

"I heard you are still exerting a lot?" PK came to know and asked me.

"Yes, I need to focus on both, remaining project work as well as the MBA," I replied.

"But you need to do a balancing act so that your body also remains rejuvenated. You need to work in such a manner that you give your best but still find time for rejuvenation," he advised.

"Excellence with Fun," I thought and said to him in agreement.

My MBA papers went exceedingly well, and I was super delighted. It was time for me to take a short trip to Lucknow and meet Anita.

I spent the next 4 days in Lucknow, and enjoyed my time with my fiancé. We roamed around the town, did a lot of shopping, went to a movie and had our moment at a friend's house. It indeed was good to know her more and spend time with her. I wanted to close the past chapters and move on to write a new chapter of my life with her.

The date of marriage was discussed. I was okay for October, as that would have been a little lean time due to the Diwali festivals and I could take more time off. Families consulted with Pandit and came out with four date options in October. I was attracted to one date 'Friday the 13th October.' In the western world Friday, the 13th is considered a haunting day. But, I had many reasons to choose this date. At first, 13th has been my lucky number and Friday has been my Lucky day, secondly, number 13 is considered to be Lord Shiva's number. So, I chose Friday the 13th of October as the date of my marriage. Time flew in Lucknow, and then I had to come back to the action in Thane.

The result of my MBA papers had come and I secured good marks in all five papers. I again thanked my stars for not pulling me down. I decided to start getting engaged in other group company projects while still supporting the IFAS project. Many projects were going on in parallel. For the next couple of months, I kept on looking after many projects, moving from one premise of a group company to the other.

In between, the head of Raymond Limited, Kenya, sent their senior leaders to visit India and look at the IT transformation projects in India. They were specifically keen to look at the IFAS application.

We met them and gave the demo of the IFAS application. The visiting leaders appreciated the application and started putting pressure to automate the finance as well as other applications of Raymond Ltd., Kenya. While, I was very keen to take that engagement due to the international exposure, yet it was not the right time to take additional projects. We assured them to consider their request soon.

My marriage time was approaching fast and I wanted to complete as much work before I leave so that the pressure is less when I return.

I left for my marriage, a week before the marriage date. I planned to take more leave after the marriage. I got married and my status changed from 'Single ready to mingle' to 'Married and got mingled.'

After the marriage, we went to Nainital, my favorite place. We spent around a week there and developed more understanding with each other besides having fun.

I was loving the romance in my favorite place, Nainital. I had a partner now, who can understand the real me and not my status. My first experience and impression were very good and fulfilling. The good time flies fast and it was my time to come back to Thane.

Since, I had shared my intentions that I may get an opportunity to work in the USA within 1.5 years, both parents wanted Anita to spend some time in Lucknow before moving to Thane. It was decided that Anita will come to Thane after a month, with my parents and sister's family.

I left for my 'Karma-bhoomi' Mumbai area alone to continue my quest.

Chapter 18

The Initiative, The Curiosity and The Opportunity

Back in Thane, my focus was on 'Excellence with Fun'.

"The Fun"

The RCS team had become a close-knit family. We all worked very hard and partied harder. Mumbai people are fun and I was enjoying this fun.

"The Excellence"

Existing projects were getting in a good shape. The real good part was that the projects were on diversified domains across group companies operating in diversified industries, like textile, steel, cement, healthcare, cosmetics, retail, etc. This gave me a fantastic rich diversified exposure to the industrial processes and various domains.

After keenly watching these group companies and the various automation processes, I observed that various department processes were linked with each other. There was duplication of the application structure. This needed more effort to design, implement and maintain each application. This was a painful thing to see. I thought why I can't create more integrated applications which will reduce duplication, reduce maintenance, and huge cost savings for the organization.

I remembered, how the Kenya leadership team was very keen on overall computerization/transformation. I discussed this basic idea, with some of my friends in the information technology field, and came to know about the Enterprise Resource Planning (ERP) concept.

Enterprise resource planning (**ERP**) is **defined** as the ability to deliver an **integrated suite of business applications.**

ERP tools share a common process and data model, covering broad and deep operational end-to-end processes like finance, manufacturing, distribution, SCM, and HR. Without knowing the concept of ERP, just as a common sense, I realized the need of the hour of a common integrated application. I learned that this is a well-established concept of ERP adopted in developed countries, I decided to discuss it with PK.

"Raymond Kenya is eager to transform all their processes. While they want their Financial Accounting applications on priority, but they also had been keen on automating their other processes like Sales Order System, Manufacturing System, Goods Delivery system, and Invoicing System. To design these applications individually, there will be a lot of duplication in the architecture besides more time and money will be spent in maintenance post Go live," I shared the thought.

"I agree. What do you propose?" he asked curiously.

"I propose that we look at the overall computerization from the ERP perspective. We draw a big picture and break that into various sub-applications, and then start developing and delivering them one by one. We can prioritize and deliver, IFAS project in phase one, as per their need, and subsequently deliver other projects to them. This will save huge time and money in the subsequent projects as well during continuous maintenance," I shared my thoughts.

"Makes sense. Sounds like a good plan," PK agreed to the overall plan.

"Fine. Let me create a proposition for the leadership team of Raymond, Kenya," I was excited about this fantastic opportunity.

It was time for Anita to come to Thane along with my parents and my younger sister's family. I was looking for an independent home. PK helped me get company accommodation in Vasant Vihar in Thane.

The flat was a very spacious 1BHK furnished flat, with a wonderful view of the small mountains. I was excited for my family to visit me in 'my home' and start the new journey of life with Anita. The day came and they arrived. I brought them from Thane station in three autos. When we reached home, everyone was very happy to see the flat and the preparation. After settling down, we realized that my father's suitcase was left in the auto itself. My father was very particular about his stuff and used to keep all important things, including cash, and important documents, in his suitcase. I felt very bad, thinking this is such a bad start. I tried very hard, to locate the auto and even reached out to the auto association, but ultimately, we could not get the suitcase. Father's mood was quite off, due to the loss of valuables. But soon we moved on and had a lot of fun. We visited all the important places in Mumbai and nearby places. Then we took a trip to Lonavala, Khandala, Panchgani, and Mahabaleshwar. It was a very fun-filled trip and I felt rejuvenated. I and Anita sent off the family.

After a while, we invited the Raymond Kenya team and shared their thoughts on developing an ERP for Raymond Kenya. They were excited and after a few discussions and deliberations gave a go-ahead. The first phase was to implement the IFAS application with alignment to the Kenya market. We started with the overall architecture and the customization of the IFAS application to meet the Kenya requirement. In a few months, we were ready with the basic system. In September 1996, we decided to do a pilot run of the customized IFAS application in Kenya. The decision was taken that I, along with Mukund Bhat, will travel to Kenya for around a month to install the application, validate the processes and then train the finance department team in Kenya. The plan was that Mukund Bhat will be transferred to Kenya to continue supporting the IFAS applications.

I was very excited as this was my first international trip. I had obtained my passport after I had planned to go to the USA, for my much-needed and planned growth. I and Mukund prepared for the trip.

I took my first international flight to Kenya. I was on the right path.

I had an image of Africa being quite underdeveloped (with exception of South Africa). I imagined Kenya also may be quite underdeveloped. The Raymond Woollen Mills Ltd. was registered in Kenya for manufacturing knitting yarns and price goods of wool and wool mixed with synthetic fibres, and woollen and worsted fabrics. Its flagship Red and Black check blankets and shawls can be seen, worn by the people living in remote tribes, across Africa, including the famous Masai tribes, living in, one of the biggest grasslands-based wildlife sanctuaries.

We landed in Kenya and stayed for a night in Nairobi. The first impression of the wide roads and good cars, gave us a big surprise, as it was different than our perception. The headquarters of Raymond Kenya was in a city called Eldoret. Eldoret is a principal town in the Rift Valley region of Kenya. The average temperature of Eldoret remains around 16-17 degrees Celsius, making it an amazing place climate-wise. The next day we took a road trip from Nairobi to Eldoret. The roads were just amazing, throughout, with all modern cars running at very high speed. Eldoret was a small town and the factory was on the outskirts. There was the complete township of Raymond with a factory and houses for its employees along with the guest house in which we stayed. Our overall perception changed. **I learned that one shall**

not make an impression based on some generic hearsay or imagination.

Mr. Gopal Chadha was the general manager and the head of the Raymond Kenya unit. The township and the guest house facilities were very good, and we started working on the project without losing time. We were told not to venture out of the secured township premises, as it was quite unsafe outside. There were incidents of looting and shootings, so we generally remained within the township. We installed the application and started validating the processes that were given to us when the Kenya officials had visited Mumbai. We learned that there were few complications besides a lot of exception scenarios, specific to Kenya. This was surprising but we fixed the problems quickly. Parallely, we started understanding other systems that needed to be developed as part of the overall integrated ERP application. We focused on three systems– Manufacturing, Sales-Invoicing, and Distribution. Since, these were complex applications and only two of us had traveled to Kenya, it was taking more time. I wanted to go back as per plan by the first week of October as my first marriage anniversary was on 13th October. But, there was a huge pressure and I was requested to stay back to complete the IFAS implementation, and complete the system study of the other systems, to give a download to the RCS team to develop the same.

I had to stay back and missed celebrating my first anniversary with Anita and she was quite disheartened with this. By October last week, we implemented the IFAS project. As a goodwill gesture, Mr. Gopal Chadha insisted that he will sponsor our trip to the Masai-Mara wildlife game reserve, which is one of the biggest in the world. We delightedly accepted the offer. I along with Mukund Bhat and two more officials from Raymond Kenya, traveled to Masai-Mara. I felt fortunate for this opportunity to see the game park, as well as the remote side of Kenya. A wildlife camp inside the game park was booked for three nights for our stay. The jeep was to take us to various locations in Masa Mara. Eldoret to Masai Mara is around an 8-hour drive. It was amazing to see the remote country landscape changing drastically from plateau to brazen land to large lakes to grasslands. After driving for 5 hours, we saw a petrol pump. The driver stopped the car to refill the fuel tank. A 6.5 feet tall native black guy came and knocked on my window. I was a little afraid due to what I had heard and looked at his physique.

"Kaemchoo," the tall black guy asked me. Swahili is the official and widely spoken language in Kenya, so I thought he is talking in Swahili.

I looked at the driver a little perplexed, since I did not know Swahili.

"He is talking to you and asking you something," the driver told me.

"But I don't know Swahili," I told the driver.

"No. No. He is talking to you in your language," the driver smiled.

I looked back perplexed at the person again and he saw my reaction.

"Keemchoo," he spoke again.

And then my tube light got switched on. He was talking in Gujarati and was asking me 'Kem Chho?' meaning 'How are you?'.

"Maja ma (I am good)," I smiled and responded to him with a huge surprise. He smiled and then started filling the fuel.

I was literally zapped, to see a native black, in one of the remotest places of Kenya, talking to me in Gujarati. I was happily surprised and a little shocked with this, thinking 'How does the guy know Gujarati?'

As we entered the grasslands of Masai Mara reserve park, it was around afternoon time. Hardly after driving for 15 minutes, we saw a big group of Ostriches running in parallel. A little farther, we started seeing huge herds of Zebra, Gazelles, Wild beasts, and various types of dears in huge numbers. It was a beautiful and delightful sight. The landscape was a mix of huge flat and slightly sloped land with trees and bushes. I could see for miles and miles. A little further ahead, we saw a mother Cheetah laying along with 5-6 cubs, on the side of a small bush. We took a lot of photos. We also saw a few large mighty African elephants. But it was a treat to eyes to see a group of Giraffes roaming in the grassland.

Around late evening, we reached our camp in the middle of the wildlife sanctuary. The camp was developed by digging around 20 feet deep circular trench which was filled with water so, it became a sort of piece of land surrounded by deep water. They had built a wooden bridge, to reach inside the camp, with security gates at both ends manned by armed guards. We reached inside the camp, and it was a beautiful wooden hut in which we had to stay. At night the wooden bridge was lifted, to cut off the camp from the main wildlife park. The atmosphere, gave us an adrenalin rush, as in the night we kept on hearing the roars of lions and other animals. It was a funny feeling of, us being inside a locked-in cage with animals roaming free outside. The next day's plan was, to leave early morning, to see big cats (lions, cheetahs, and leopards) killing if we are lucky, as they generally hunt late at night or early morning. In the atmosphere of excitement, it was very difficult to sleep.

The next day, we left in a jeep, and after hardly 30 minutes of wandering, seeing many animals, we saw three big

African mane lions, with huge beards, resting in a place. On approaching close, we saw a killed animal lying in between them. The lions were sitting on three different sides from the corpse, around 20-30 meters apart. Our driver took the jeep from the fourth open side and stopped hardly 3-4 meters from the corpse. We were stunned by his move and were scared although we were inside the closed jeep. We looked and realized that it was a dead hyena probably killed by these lions. One of the lions got up and walked close to our jeep. We took photos. The driver then pulled back around 20-25 meters and stopped. The lion seemed a little upset, he went back to the corpse of the dead hyena and took the body in his mouth, from around the ribs area, and started crushing. We could hear the distinct voice of bone-crunching. It was a very scary scene. The lion then moved back to his previous location and sat down. We waited there for a while viewing this magnificent scene. After a while, an open jeep with an antenna, with two park rangers in it, came and stopped right next to the hyena. We felt the guy is making a stupid mistake, stopping an open jeep between three lions sitting around the corpse. The lions stared looking curiously at the jeep. Before we could understand anything one of the rangers got down with a speed of light, and pulled the dead hyena from one leg, and jumped in the back of the open jeep. We saw it was a white female. Our heart came into our mouth, and we thought that the lion will jump and attack the rangers. Before lions could react, the male ranger started moving the jeep in the reverse direction. Two lions got up and started running behind the jeep. We realized at that point that the rangers were making a film of this whole thing. After a while, the lions stopped and the rangers also stopped at a distance. It was the craziest and scariest thing I had ever seen in person in the wildlife. The next day, we saw a leopard trying to take the seemingly freshly killed corpse of a Gazelle, upon a tree. It was quite a scene. I felt very lucky as people had told me that seeing killings by big cats was not easy at all. And we had already seen two killings by big cats. On our last day in the park, we saw a Rhinoceros and a few other animals too. Around afternoon time, we spotted five adult cheetahs having fun with each other. After a little while, they quietly sat and started watching in a direction. We took our jeep a little ahead, from the side, and saw a big herd of gazelles grazing. The landscape had a little slope and the gazelles were at the bottom of the slope, around 200 meters from the cheetahs. In the next one hour, we saw the perfect strategy built and executed by the cheetahs. Two started moving very slowly on the right side and the two on the left side while one approached from the front. They were crawling for a few steps and then stopping to not get detected and then again moving. When they reached close to the herd, they launched the full-speed attack. The heard got confused seeing the cheetahs coming from different directions. In this moment of confusion, they ran in different directions. The cheetah running from the middle killed one gazelle, and one more was killed by the other cheetahs. It was amazing to watch the perfect strategy and execution. The trip was amazing and we felt very lucky to see all the three big cat killings besides watching all the major animals of the grassland. We came back totally satisfied.

On sharing the incident about the black guy speaking to me in Gujrati, Mr. Gopal Chadha shared that the major economy in Kenya is in the hands of Gujarati businessmen for years and hence common Gujrati words are well known here. This was a big surprise to me but I felt very proud.

It was time to go back to Mumbai.

Chapter 19

Keep an eye on opportunities

It was already the end of October in 1996, and I had completed around one year and eight months in RCS and had only around four months left for my two years commitment given to PK. The 'Rebel' in me was very much alive and kicking, and so was my 'Retaliation'. I was very determined to go to the USA and achieve the respectable height of success. I had learned a lot, made major achievements, got success, and was very confident. I felt ready to make my mark in the USA. In the meanwhile, I had completed all theory papers of MBA and had received, Diploma, Advance Diploma and Specialization certificates already in a step-by-step manner. Now, I needed to submit the final project report, to get my MBA degree as well. Though, my approach towards my target has been very aggressive, I worked hard to achieve these targets, and I was on track and getting the required results. I thanked my stars again.

With the success of the IFAS project in Kenya, things were looking good for me. I gave the download of the Raymond Kenya visit to PK. I also shared the progress on the system study of the other applications, part of the overall ERP. We created a plan to develop and implement these applications. I specifically requested PK, to put some senior leads on these applications so that they can get the opportunity to travel and implement these applications. I reminded him that my two years are getting over in around four months and I am planning to look for opportunities in the USA. He appreciated my transparency and advance intimation.

I started looking for USA opportunities. My expertise was in SYBASE and Power builder area. I had heard that these skill-sets were in demand in the USA and one can get an opportunity easily with these skill-sets. Many companies based in the SEEPZ (Santacruz Electronics Export Processing Zone) area of Mumbai were sending resources on a work visa to the USA. One such opportunity was offered by a company, called MelStar, based in SEEPZ. I went to meet them and after the first round of interviews, they gave me the offer for a position of SYBASE DBA in the USA with very good remuneration. I was asked to submit my passport to apply for a work visa (H1B) processing which I submitted subsequently.

I felt super happy and overwhelmed for securing a job in the USA.

The 'Rebel' in me was happy and emotional to see the 'Retaliation' going in the right direction. "People can't say now that I am a failure."

With the excitement and expectation of moving to the USA, I started thinking about completing the pending tasks in India, like completing my MBA project and taking the ongoing projects in Raymond to a logical conclusion/handover. I did not want to do injustice to any task.

"I got the offer from MelStar for the position of SYBASE DBA in the USA," I informed PK.

"Fantastic, congratulations," he sounded happy.

"This was quick. What is the timeline to join?" he was curious.

"They are starting my work visa (H1B) filing process. I think this should take at least 2-3 months," I replied as per my understanding.

"Ok then let us take the status of all the projects, and see how best we can plan on each project, to either complete before you leave, or plan the proper handover," he suggested.

"Sure Boss," I responded.

Next few days, we did the status review meeting of various projects. We identified the projects that can be completed within the next two months, and also those projects where we need to identify my successors, for proper planning and handover. We had estimated that my expected last day in Raymond will be the end of January, which meant that I had around two months now. The major focus was to complete Kenya projects, since, I had done the system study, and had brought the knowledge to develop these applications. We created the plan for all three applications and I started working with the teams.

"Sudeep, you need to go to Kenya one last time to ensure things go right," PK came and asked me after a few days.

"But I am waiting for my visa," I hesitated.

"That is fine, we will be back within two weeks so don't worry about that," he assured me.

"But MelStar has taken my passport also," I shared my concern.

"How can they take your passport. For H1B visa processing they don't need it. Once the visa is processed, then to get visa stamped, you need to go to the US Consulate with your passport," PK was surprised.

"I was told that many people apply for the visa and companies spend money to process visa. And many times, when a visa comes, people do not get it stamped, and instead, opt for another better offer that they get in between. So, as a surety, these companies ask to submit the passport, to ensure that the resource does not ditch them," I explained the reason that was told to me.

"Ok, in that case, I will talk to the seniors in MelStar, and get back the passport for Kenya visit," PK expressed his intention.

PK wanted to go to Kenya, once along with me, just to ensure that he also has a grip on the projects before my exit.

"Sure, we will go together any day you want to," I agreed.

We met the senior leader in MelStar. After meeting PK, and hearing the situation, MelStar leader agreed and handed back the passport to us. The flight to Kenya was booked for the subsequent week.

The demand for Indian resources was growing very fast, and almost every other day, my friends and colleagues used to go for interviews. I was enjoying my time since the tension to find a job in the USA was not my concern anymore. I did have anxiety about my visa processing. I used to tag along with friends for such job interviews, for fun sake, because my interest was to go to the movie after their interviews and have fun. This was a regular practice and we enjoyed it a lot.

"We are going for an interview in Seepz tomorrow. Would you like to come? After that we will watch a movie and roam around Fashion Street," one of my friends asked me one day.

"Sure. It's a weekend so we can go," I replied.

My friend had his walk-in-interview at the Foundation Software in SEEPZ. I told my friend that I will wait outside, while he can give an interview. It was a humid day so when we reached there, I decided to wait at the reception instead of waiting outside. At the reception, they announced that there will be a written test before the interviews. I decided to give walk in test instead of waiting at the reception to keep myself busy. I gave the test after and was shortlisted. They started the interview. Towards the end, they told me that they will inform the results after a few days. I informed them about my two weeks Kenya plan, and that I can be reached there. I gave my Raymond Kenya guest house address and phone number and left.

I took the flight to Kenya once again, in December 1996, along with PK and two other team members who were taking over the other projects for final implementation. After reaching Kenya, we took deep dive into the details of each project. Things were looking good from the project execution perspective. We worked very hard and at the same time, since we had good company, we had good fun in the evenings (Excellence with Fun was continuing).

One day we got a call, in the guest house, from India and I was informed that it was for me.

"Sudeep, you have been selected based on our interactions a few days back," the Foundation Software professional informed me on the call.

"Oh, thanks. What is the location of the assignment?" I asked.

"It is for our Singapore office," the person responded.

"Oh, I am extremely sorry but I already have an offer from the USA now and that is where I want to go," I apologized. "How can I go to Singapore when I already have an offer from the USA?" I thought.

The person heard from the other side and after a little pause spoke. "We also have a big operation in North America, primarily in the USA. Give me a couple of days and I will get back to you to see if we can have an opportunity for you in the USA," the person informed me. "Sure, thank you so much for your consideration," I closed the call.

I shared the details of my discussion, with PK, after the call.

"What is the technology they are hiring for," PK asked.

"PeopleSoft," I informed him.

"What is PeopleSoft?" PK enquired.

"Honestly, I don't know as I gave this interview for fun," I told him the actual reason for the interview.

"But if a technology is needed, both in Singapore and US, there must be some good opportunity in this," he was curious. "Let us at least understand what is PeopleSoft, before you say no to them, even if you are thinking that," he said logically.

“Sure Boss, makes sense,” I agreed that at least we should know.

We searched and found that PeopleSoft is an ERP. We also found that there were jobs with high hourly rates available in PeopleSoft. This seemed very interesting and made me very curious.

“This is very interesting. Let us call someone, in the USA, and ask them about the scope of PeopleSoft,” PK wanted to find out.

We called one of the ex-Raymond colleagues who moved to the USA.

“How come you got an offer of PeopleSoft in India?” he was surprised.

“I have got the offer from Foundation Software, who are partners of PeopleSoft Inc. USA. They are training people in India and then sending them to their subsidiaries in USA and Singapore” I explained.

“You should just close your eyes and take the offer immediately,” the person sounded surprised and emphasized to take the offer.

“PeopleSoft is one of the most popular ERPs nowadays and its demand is growing exponentially in the USA. Being an ERP, it’s highly niche technology and application. The career growth on PeopleSoft will be exponential,” he now shared the perspective on PeopleSoft.

This Advice was an eye-opener for all of us. I could not believe what I just heard. I wanted to go to the USA but the offer is for Singapore.

“Sudeep, we have considered your request and we are glad to inform you that you have been selected for our USA operations. You need to join us by mid-Jan,” the Foundation person called and informed us.

"Thank you. I am accepting your offer for the USA. I will join by the required date," I immediately accepted the offer and confirmed.

'What has just happened with me?' I asked myself with surprise.

My ignorance of the 'in-demand technology could have devoid me from the path of much needed exponential growth. It was PK, who was curious, and hence we did enquire in detail about PeopleSoft and found about the value of the actual opportunity.

The Advice to take the PeopleSoft opportunity was the best, for the 'Rebel' in me to take my 'Retaliation' to its final destination quickly.

I just got another major learning of my lie:

- **There are so many opportunities in the market but often we either do not know about them or miss them due to our ignorance or lack of knowledge.**
- **Never ignore the opportunities passing around you.**
- Be curious to explore the opportunity before making a decision.
- Talk to seniors and people in the network to understand what is happening in market and identify upcoming futuristic opportunities.
- Being complacent with an in-hand growth opportunity may result in missing bigger opportunities.
- Opportunities with high demand & low supply; niche technology; sustained future demand takes you on a higher growth path.

Chapter 20

The Boot Camp

I joined Foundation Technology, and the plan was to go through rigorous training for around 3 months on PeopleSoft, post which, we were to be placed in various projects in the USA. The training program was called 'The Boot Camp' and I heard this term for the first time.

Later, I learned that the term, Boot Camp, was adopted from the term "boot" originated from US Navy and Marine recruits in the Spanish–American War (1898) who wore leggings called boots. These recruits were trained in "boot" camps. **Boot camp** refers to the initial instruction of new military personnel. Our Boot Camp was focused in such a manner that in a minimal time of three months we were supposed to learn about the complete PeopleSoft ERP application. An ERP application, is very complex, with its design, architecture, technology, and functional application for various domains.

PeopleSoft applications have modules that large corporations use to effectively manage human resources (HRMS), customer relationships (CRM), financial and supply chains (FSCM), enterprise performance (EPM), and Campus Solutions (CS). Additionally, PeopleSoft has its proprietary development toolset, called PeopleTools.

Three months to learn so many things, was indeed a rigorous exercise and quickly we understood why it was named Boot Camp. There were nine people in our batch. Four of them were selected for US assignments (Sameer Munje, Ramesh Gopal, Advait Deshpande, and myself), and the other four for the Singapore (Mitesh Raut, Nitesh Vadgama, Venu Iyer, and Harki) and one Indian person (Seema Powar).

In parallel, I started working on finalizing my project for the MBA program. I had taken the topic of Integrated Financial Accounting System (IFAS) as this was my practical learning as well in Raymond, and the course demanded practical learning. I was required to opt for a project guide as per the guidelines of the university. I identified Mr. Vasanthrajan (Head of Accounts Receivable in Raymond) with whom I had worked closely on the IFAS project earlier. Study center folks accepted his profile. I started preparing the project report.

Time flies, when one is busy and happy. Two months of training were completed in a flash, and it was only a month left to fly to the USA. My adrenalin rush was increasing.

In the late 1990s, many Indians had started going to the USA for work, yet it was very prestigious and not considered very easy. Back home in Lucknow, my family members were very happy about my growth and achievement so far but were very nervous as well as excited, for my upcoming move to the USA. My mother was especially very happy that I was nearing my target. Her main concern was my happiness and she knew the angst in me. 'Mothers know it all,' I smiled thinking about my mother. My sister was happy but a little nervous about my not-so-fluent spoken English. My determination did not see any of that.

There was huge excitement as many people, from the previous batch, had already started leaving for various opportunities in USA and Singapore. It gave us a good feeling that our turn will also come soon.

"Sudeep, you have been selected to join the Sears Roebuck and Company in Chicago," the head of the center informed me.

"Wow. Thank you so much," I was excited to hear about Chicago.

"We will give you a different offer letter that of the US Entity of Foundation Software and its terms and conditions. You need to accept that," he said and I was given a new offer letter from a US entity.

"You need to get your visa stamped and fly to the US and join our headquarters in New York on 22nd April next month," he continued.

"After the joining formalities in New York, you have to fly to Chicago, the next day, as that will be your base city. Your first assignment will be with Sears Roebuck and Company in Chicago," he continued.

"Your visa has come and you need to get it stamped at the US Consulate in Mumbai. Plan your next steps now," he concluded.

"Thank you so much. I will get my visa stamped first and then will do my preparations," I responded happily and with excitement.

I and Sameer Munje were to fly on the same flight. The other two persons of the batch for the USA were to fly next month.

We decided that I will fly alone to the USA and call Anita after I get settled in 2-3 months. This way, I will be able to plan accommodation and other essentials, and I can settle in the work environment before she comes. This meant that Anita will have to travel alone to Chicago, later. Anita had never taken a flight till then. I decided to make her fly alone from Mumbai to Lucknow to gain some experience of traveling alone on a flight and handling things at the airport. Anita decided to take the flight to Lucknow, the day after my flight to the USA.

I finalized my project report on IFAS for MBA and submitted it along with the project guide resume and recommendation at the university. I felt accomplished completing this task too.

Sameer and I were flying together to New York as his assignment was in New York itself. At the airport, around 35-40 people came to see us off. From Sameer's house alone, around 25 people came, from my side 5 persons including Anita and 8-10 colleagues from Foundation. It was a large gathering at the airport and we felt excited yet emotional.

We boarded the British Airways flight to London on way to New York.

Chapter 21

I was on my first flight to the USA, my dream destination. 'The Rebel' inside me had converted the anger into excitement. 'The Retaliation' was tasting the sweetness of success with this flight.

Travelling is in my blood and I loved traveling. My grandfather, Satya Charan Shastri, was an elite educationist, a freedom fighter, an Aryasamaji, and an avid traveler. He was the principal of the famous DAV college in Gorakhpur. He was a leader of the Indian National Congress as he wanted to promote education and the Indian value system. He worked closely with Subhash Chandra Bose and Jawahar Lal Nehru. He promoted Aryasamaj in many countries, where the ex-pat Indian population had migrated, like West Indies, Surinam, etc. He loved traveling. My father too was an avid traveler and he was very lucky to have got a career of his choice, which revolved around travel. He worked in the tourism department and retired as joint director of UP Tourism. I used to tag along with him on many official trips.

Like them, I also loved traveling. I felt that this is one legacy that I would want to carry forward. Before taking my flight, my father told me about his experience of New York and Washington DC when he traveled there, many decades ago. It felt good hearing his experience.

In my anxiety, many memories flashed in front of me. I took the status check of 'The Rebel' and 'The Retaliation' – 'How is it going?'

I was on the right path, and had made significant achievements in recent years, so 'The Rebel' in me was feeling relatively better. I looked back and thought that I was constantly getting acknowledgment and recognition in Raymond

Cement, World Bank Monitoring Cell, Technical Education Department, and recently in Raymond Consultancy. The quantum of anger had moderately reduced with the progress and, the recognition that I was getting in last few years. And now, I am on my way to the USA to take my retaliation to its final stage. For the first time after my M.Sc. debacle, I was feeling ecstatic, being on the right track. I wanted to shout in happiness 'Yes, I am there. I did it,' but I could not with so many people around in the plane.

"Five years in the USA and then, I will move back to India as I want to be with my parents in their old age. I also want to see the reaction on the faces of those people of society who had criticized, ridiculed, and ruled me out," I told myself.

In the journey, I was constantly watching the landscape down from my window seat in the airplane, as I had always been very curious about the geography and the landscapes of various places. We reached London and the view of London city was amazing from the plane, something I had not seen earlier. The kid inside me was jumping in excitement with each such view and moment. After a gap of around four hours in London, we took another British Airways flight to New York. The airplane flew over Greenland and I was amazed to see the ice-capped landscape. As we approached New York, I was overjoyed and again wanted to shout in happiness but controlled myself.

As we landed in New York, my smile was overflowing. It was amazing to see a big airport like JFK in New York. After the immigration and luggage collection, we came out at the pick-up point. Sameer knew someone in New York who came to pick him. I was told that there will be a taxi waiting for me outside near the pickup area. But, I could not see any taxi. I eagerly kept on waiting for my taxi. There was a big black limousine parked in front of the gate and this was the first time I saw such a big car in reality. I had seen such a car in some of the English movies before but not in reality. A tall 6.5 feet tall black guy in a black suit was waiting for someone to come out of the airport and was very restless. I was waiting for a while now and was getting a little concerned about the taxi. We looked at each other couple of times but did not say anything. After a few minutes when we looked at each other, I gave him a courtesy smile. He came to me and asked "You Veerma?" Since he sounded my name, I told him my name.

"Oh man, I have been waiting for you," he said a little perplexed as to why I have not asked about the taxi.

"But I was waiting for a taxi," I responded in surprise.

"That's the car for you," he said pointing to the limousine.

And before I could say anything else, he took my large luggage bags like a piece of the toy in his both giant hands and put them in the trunk of his limousinc. I was super surprised to see the limousine and the way he picked my large, heavy luggage bags like a piece of paper.

'Wow, is this the taxi for me?' was the big question in my mind.

Just to make sure, I checked about Foundation Software and the destination address, and he confirmed the same. I was completely overwhelmed. The inside view of the limousine was amazing with long space and the seat on both sides. There was a bar inside as well. Once again, I wanted to shout in excitement but, once again I had to keep quiet. He took me to the guest house to dump the luggage. "Please be ready in the next 30 minutes. I will come to pick you and take you to your office," the driver told, after dropping me at the guest house. I quickly put my luggage in the guest house, took a quick bath, and got ready within 30 minutes. I came out and the driver was waiting.

"I am ready, let's go," I waved at him.

Foundation Software headquarter was on the 79th floor of the World Trade Centre 1 (WTC-1). Reaching there, meant going into the heart of Manhattan. My eyes were wide open to see the big buildings. The kid inside me was constantly jumping with excitement, and The Rebel had disappeared. The driver dropped me in front of the WTC.

I got inside the World Trade Centre. And saw two elevators in a huge lobby, with a very high ceiling. As, I stepped inside the elevator, it started moving at a very high speed. I reached the 79th floor in almost no time. I found our office and as I entered, I saw a very nice reception surrounded by a huge open lobby.

"How can I help you?" Suzane came to the reception and asked me.

"My name is Sudeep Verma. I have come from India….," I was saying.

"Oh! Yes, yes… we were expecting you," she interrupted.

"How was your flight? Hope you are comfortable after such a long flight," she continued. I gave her a thumbs up with a smile.

"Right now, the leaders are in a meeting, so please wait here," she showed me Sofas and chairs in the big open lobby area.

"Sure, thanks," I smiled and thanked her.

I moved towards the open lobby area, and I saw big long glass walls. As I reached near it, I saw the big and wide view of Manhattan from the 79th floor of the WTC. It was a mesmerizing view with mushroomed tall buildings with lights, a network of roads, and the sea at a close distance. It was a treat to the eyes and just like the view from a Hollywood movie. The kid inside me was constantly jumping wanting to shout, "yes!, I have done it!" But it was inappropriate. I kept on watching that amazing view for 45 minutes without realizing it.

"Sudeep, the leaders will see you now," Suzane came and told me.

"Welcome to Foundation," Alag Arasan, the leader of Foundation Software, greeted me.

"Thank you so much for everything," I genuinely sounded excited.

"Let us finish the joining formality and then we will go for dinner".

"Sure, thanks," I responded.

'So, they will take me to dinner as well. What an out of the world experience, I am getting,' I thought with happiness.

After joining formalities, I was briefed about my project in Chicago.

"Sears Roebuck and Company is one of the biggest organizations in the United States. Are you aware of the fact, that the Sears Towers in downtown Chicago, is the tallest building in the world?" he asked me.

"I do understand that Sears is a big company with its operations in multiple industries. But I was not aware of the Sears Towers," I candidly accepted my ignorance.

"It is a very big customer for us and we are eager to grow this account. We are looking forward to your performance which will help us grow our presence there," Alag Arasan had set the expectations.

"Rest assured; I will give my best. I will initially understand their way of working as this is my first experience in the US," I responded.

"I am sure you will shine and we will grow that account," he said.

"Let us proceed for the dinner now. We will go to 'Shaan', the Indian restaurant on 53rd street," Alag Arasan informed me.

We left for dinner. By now it was night-time, and we stepped out of the World Trade Centre. The overwhelming night scene outside, with buildings and lights, was amazing. I had seen New York on television and in movies but watching it with naked eyes was just mesmerizing.

After the dinner, I was dropped at the guest house. I still could not shout out of happiness in the guest house as there were many other people in different rooms. I tried to sleep as I had a 6 AM flight to Chicago the next morning, but the overwhelming experience till now and the excitement about my first project kept me awake till late.

Chapter 22

I boarded the 6 AM flight, from JFK airport in New York, to the O'Hare airport in Chicago. I was flying alone this time. As usual, I took the window seat in excitement as, I wanted to see the landscape below. Once we approached Chicago, the big city landscape was visible below. When, I came out of the plane, I met with an amazing view. More than an airport it looked like a very big posh mall with shops. I saw people playing music (trumpet, drums, guitar). I was mesmerized by what I was seeing, just like a grand movie show. O'Hare is the world's busiest airport. I was thanking God that after testing me severely for years, He was rewarding my patience and perseverance.

I boarded the taxi and reached my hotel, Redroof Inn, in Schaumburg. Schaumburg, is a northwest posh suburb of Chicago in the state of Illinois. I was booked at this hotel due to its proximity to Hoffman Estates, where the headquarter of Sears Roebuck and Company is located, and where I had to report the next day.

"Yes, Yes, I did it," I shouted aloud with full volume as soon as I checked in my room. The kid in me had suppressed his excitement for a long time. I finally got the opportunity to express my happiness.

'Tring Tring Tring Tring…' The phone in my room rang shortly.

"Hello," I replied.

"Sir, is there any problem? There was a noise from your room." The lady from the reception had called to enquire.

I felt embarrassed and said shyly "No, there is no problem. All is well."

I disconnected, realizing that, the kid had shouted pretty loudly.

The next day morning, I got ready and took a taxi to the Sears office at Hoffman Estates. After driving for about 10 minutes, we took an exit from the highway and entered a driveway called Sears Parkway. We drove in a beautiful laid-down green landscape, and crossed lakes with swans floating in them. Finally, we approached a massive glass building, and the taxi stopped in front of that. When I reached inside the building, I was greeted with a phenomenal view. There was a huge hall with a height equivalent to 5-6 floors, covered with trees on the sides and running water bodies, and various stalls. After moving a few steps, I saw a group of people playing jazz music with Band, Guitar, Trumpet, etc. It was an amazing treat for the eyes and ears. However, I wondered where is the office as this seems more like a huge mall. I located a help desk and approached there, and told the lady that I have come to join Sear. I showed her, the name of my Sears manager and her address. The lady guided me to one corner of the building and explained to me where I needed to go. I reached the floor and met my new manager, Deborah Brown.

"Hi my name is Sudeep Verma and I came here to join the project today," I met Deborah and introduce myself to her.

"Oh yes, we were expecting you today," she said smiling.

"How are you doing? Did you arrive today from India?" she asked.

"No, I landed in New York yesterday and, after few formalities at my office, I took the flight to Chicago this morning," I replied smiling.

"Good. Let me give you a brief of the project and then I will show you your workplace," she spoke.

She explained, about the PeopleSoft HRMS implementation project for various group companies of Sears. She took me to a large enclosed area with an entry point, where on four corners there were four workstations. Two persons, one lady, and one gentleman were sitting on two corners. While the remaining two workstations were empty.

"This will be your workplace." She directed me to one of the empty workstations and told me.

She introduced me to the two persons sitting on the other workstations. I realized they were very senior experienced PeopleSoft functional persons, and were not technical persons like me.

"Take your time to settle in and then I will introduce you to the other key persons of the project and will show you other important places in the office." She suggested in a question mark manner.

"I am fine, I can come with you now if that's ok with you." I dropped my office bag on my workstation and told her.

"Sure, let's go." She started walking out of the cubical area.

She showed me the conference room, meeting rooms, snacks room where one can take coffee, side tables where many snacks like donuts, cakes, muffins were kept for anyone to take. I was surprised, as I had seen such type of atmosphere and freebies, for the first time in an office. Then she introduced me to some of the key project team members, with whom I needed to interact in due course of time.

The rest of the day was spent in the formality of establishing my workstation, security, authorizations, and reading some of the documents about the project. By 5 PM the office was almost empty, as people started leaving office from 4 PM onwards itself. I was surprised, to see people leaving so early. I also left the office at 5:15 PM after Deborah left, overwhelmed with my first day in the office.

The next day, I reached the office, sharp at 7:55 AM, and saw the office almost full. I learned that people come early to the office and leave early as well. I went to Deborah's office and reported to her.

"I am all set now. Please do let me know what I need to do?" I asked.

"Sure. I will come to your workplace in a little bit and will share the work plan," she responded.

"Sure, I will wait," I nodded and returned to my seat.

After about 15 minutes, she came and handed me a set of papers.

"This is the specification of an SQR program that needs to be developed. Please go through it and let me know if you have any questions." She spoke and left after my nod.

I was very excited as well as nervous to see what has been given to me, as this was my very first assignment in a new project in new technology, in a new company and that too far away in a new city and new country. The first thing I saw, was the timeline assigned for the program was 40 hours to be completed in 5 days. I started reading the specifications and got very confused.

What is this? The program looks very easy and can be developed within 3-4 hours max,' I was thinking after assessing the program.

'But how come they have allocated 40 hours for such an easy program? Am I missing something?' I started questioning myself.

I looked at the program 3-4 times and concluded that it is easy to program and there must be some kind of error in allocating the time.

I started developing the program and finished it within 3.5 hours. Then just to make sure that I have not made any mistake, I thoroughly tested it. I decided to share it with Deborah.

"I have completed the program," I informed Deborah.

"What do you mean you have completed it?" she sounded very surprised and looked at me suspiciously.

"The program was very easy, so I finished it," I told her shyly.

"Are you sure? How can that be? Was this program already coded somewhere?" she was still not able to understand how a program, estimated for 40 hours, can be developed in less than 4 hours.

"No, I have developed it from the scratch. But if you want, I can check it again one more time." I told her.

"Ok," she said suspiciously still confused over what has happened.

I came back to my desk and thought, "am I missing anything?"

"I cannot afford to screw my very first assignment." I got a little worried and nervous and started looking at the program very carefully once again. Even after reviewing it 4-5 times, again and again, I did not find anything that I had missed. The program seemed very easy.

"Let me call someone in the night and check if I am making any mistake," I decided not to submit it due to my lack of confidence.

I came back to the hotel, after work hours, and called one of my senior colleagues in Foundation who was placed in a different project.

"Don't worry you seem to have written the right program." After my explanation, he confirmed with me and started laughing.

"I have seen this many a times. The estimations here are highly enlarged," He shared his experience. "You go ahead and submit the program confidently tomorrow morning," he gave me confidence.

"Thanks. Good night," I appreciated his inputs and felt confident.

The next day morning, after taking the printout of the test results in the office, I went straight to Debora's cabin.

"The program was really simple and I had finished it yesterday and as per our discussions, I have checked it again and it is working fine. Here are the test results as well," I told Deborah slightly with confidence.

"That is very fast but let me get it checked. I will get back to you," she replied. I could still see surprise and doubt in her eyes.

I came back to my desk. I did not have anything else to do, so I just waited restlessly. When one is free, the mind wanders in all directions. I was very anxious about the outcome of my program.

"I hope I have not screwed up. I hope they do not find any problem and throw me out of the project," I kept thinking with typical anxiety and a lack of self-confidence, in which we Indians think in general.

"The program is right, Sudeep. But how did you develop it so quickly?" Deborah came and informed me with a surprise on her face.

"I found it very easy so, I developed it quickly, and I was not sure why 40 hours was allocated for this very easy task. I thought there may be a typing mistake in the estimations," I told her.

"When you sounded surprised yesterday, I thought, I may be missing something. Hence, I checked it multiple times, including testing with the test data as well," I smiled with relief and shared my thoughts.

"I understand," She smiled.

"Any other work for me, please," I asked.

"Unfortunately, I cannot allocate you anything now, since the current schedule is planned according to the current estimations, but I will try to allocate you something tomorrow," she said and left with a smile.

"My first task has been successful; I am not going back to India. I am here to stay and succeed," I heaved a big sigh of relief and smiled.

Chapter 23

Self Confidence and Courage

After the success of the first program, I was allocated the next program the next day, and the same thing happened this time as well. The time allocated for the program was 40 hours, and I finished it within 5 hours and submitted it to Deborah.

"Was this one easy too?" she was not surprised and asked smiling.

"Yes, this too was very easy, and to remove any doubts, I have tested it a few times and have attached the printouts of the test results.

"Thanks a lot, Sudeep. I will try to allocate some other work to you but since this month's chart allocation has already happened, I am not sure if I can give you more work but, in the meanwhile, you can read some of the documentation which will help you with the processes." She explained her situation to me. In-office, the work was going at a very slow pace. Deborah was impressed with my work but was still going as per the planned work schedule for the month.

Foundation had arranged a three-week hotel stay for me, so that I can get adjusted, to the project as well as the place, and within that duration, find my accommodation. I started looking for a rental apartment. I liked 'The Village in The Park' apartment complexes on Valley Lake Drive in Schaumburg. This was a 1BHK apartment but very spacious. I chose the flat on the ninth floor as the view from the windows was amazing with the Lake and a forest area visible. I signed the lease agreement and moved into the apartment. The apartment had all the utilities like a refrigerator, cooking unit, chimney, dishwasher, microwave, and oven, etc. I needed to purchase furniture.

After around three weeks in office, Deborah walked in with a very fat, overweight, bald, and short height guy who must have been in the 50-55 years of age group. She allocated him the last empty workstation, in our enclosed area. After the person settled in, he was introduced to us as John. Now our area was fully occupied.

"Sudeep, I need you to do something and keep it only up to you," Deborah took me to a meeting room and asked me in confidence.

"Sure, please tell me," I asked.

"I am giving you around 90 specifications where the estimation to develop each program has been done. I want you to do your assessment of time estimation to develop a program on each of these specifications. Do not get biased with the given time-estimations," She clarified her intention that she want me to validate the estimations.

"Sure, I will be happy to do as this will keep me engaged," I smiled.

"Please keep this strictly with yourself as I want to understand if this difference of time-estimation is only for some specific programs or in general for all of the programs," she further clarified.

"I completely understand and will keep it to myself," I assured her.

I started the assessment. As I progressed, I became more and more surprised, to see that almost all the programs were estimated, with almost 5-10 times more than my estimations.

'Why? Maybe the person, was not good in programming?' I thought.

I completed all the estimations in a few days and went to Deborah.

"I have completed the estimations," I informed her.

"Almost all the estimations are hugely inflated with much higher estimated time," I told her and gave further details. "Here is the summarised sheet with the program, estimations given and my relative estimation time. I think there is some gross mistake in these estimations," I elaborated and expressed my concern as well.

"Thank you so much for your quick revert as always. I will get it looked at. And please do not share this with anyone," she reminded again.

"Sure Deborah, be rest assured," I gave her confidence.

"Something is seriously wrong. I hope I do not get in trouble," I thought.

I noticed that John used to be quite restless and kept rotating his chair with unease. Due to his very heavy body, the chair used to make discomforting noises. As a result, my focus used to go to John and his chair, quite often. In such moments our eyes used to meet, and I used to just smile, nod, and then quickly turn around, to face my computer.

One day, he seemed very restless and was rotating a lot sitting in his chair, and when I looked in his direction, our eyes met again.

"Hi John, any problem?" I asked out of courtesy.

"Well, yes. Can you help me?" he asked.

"What is it?" I asked curiously.

"Can you have a look at this program please?" he requested for help.

"Sure, let me look at it," I accepted to help him.

I walked to his desk and looked at the specification closely. Then I looked at the program he was writing. I was very surprised to see how did he write the program. John was a very senior person almost double my age. But the program was very basic with many programming logic as well as technical mistakes.

"I think you missed a few things, let me show you," I pointed to errors.

"Thank you so much So-deep (his pronunciation)," he felt obliged.

"No problem at all," I said and returned to my desk.

I was very surprised about what I had just seen.

In the next couple of weeks, he started asking for my help more and more. Though, I was surprised about his asking for help, yet I was also happy as I had started getting more work in my relatively free time. A few times, I ended up writing the whole program for him. My focus was to learn more and more in minimal time. I kept on helping him.

"Can I buy you lunch today So-deep?" John felt obliged and requested me after a few weeks.

"Oh no need for that," I said smiling.

"I would love to," he insisted.

"Ok sure, as you wish," I agreed.

We went to the cafeteria. The cafeteria in the Sear building was spread in a huge area, where there were different sections for different types of food, American, Mexican, Chinese, Italian, Japanese and Indian, etc. There was a sitting area inside the huge covered restaurant area as well as outside in front of a lake with white swans. This was an amazing restaurant and it was a good rejuvenation for me.

"What will you take?" John asked.

"I will go for a chicken burger and fries," I told him.

"Sounds good. I will go for that too," he nodded his head.

John gave the order and made the payment. We then collected our burger and fries and sat on chairs across the table, facing each other.

"Thanks, John, for the meal," I smiled and thanked him.

"My pleasure. You are my savior," he expressed his gratitude.

We started eating the meal and did not speak much during that time. After finishing the meal, I decided to start the conversation.

"Where were you working before this project, John?" I asked as that was the typical conversational question that came to my mind.

"I was painting," he replied with a calmness.

I got confused for a moment with his response.

I thought he may have worked in a specialized software related to the painting which I have never heard of. That's why he is struggling in PeopleSoft. Even I was not aware of PeopleSoft till sometime back.

"Which application or software you were working on related to painting?" I asked him curiously.

He understood my confusion and laughed aloud.

"No, no, I had my own painting work, and I was painting houses and buildings," he replied, laughing. His heavy body and bald face shining.

I was zapped, completely speechless. He saw my face and continued.

"I was getting 20-25 dollars per hour in my job, even after working for more than 30 years now. And I used to hear that the young software programmers are earning 100-200 dollars per hour. I thought, what the fuck, let me also get into this programming stuff. I did a computer programming course for six months and here I am," he revealed.

I was further surprised, zapped, and speechless, by what I had heard. But inside me, 'my inner self' stood up and gave a BIG SALUTE to him.

This was very big learning of COURAGE, for me.

At the age of over 50 years, this person had the courage, took the challenge, and decided to learn something completely different than what he had been doing for over 30 years. And he did not get bothered with what others will think about it and how hard it will be to learn something entirely different. He had the guts to do it and here he is.

'It is never too late to take a challenge and learn something new.'
"COURAGE GIVES RESULTS."
"NOTHING IS IMPOSSIBLE."

Chapter 24

More than two months had passed for me in the United States. I was depending on my colleagues, friends, or taxies for my daily commute between office and home. In the United States, survival is very difficult without a car, and I wanted to change this situation quickly. I needed a car, but before that, I needed a driving license in the United States.

My friends informed me about the two agencies, in the Schaumburg area, which give driving lessons and help in getting a driving license– 'Bombay Driving School' and 'Delhi Driving School'. I laughed hearing Indian driving schools in the USA. I called Mr. Patel in Delhi driving school and took '5 classes + help in getting DL' deal at a minimal price.

Patel came in his training car on Saturday morning, and I started driving with ease because the car was automatic. I was very careful while driving as in the US as the vehicles follow the 'Right-hand drive' rule, unlike the 'Left-hand drive' rule in India which the Britishers had introduced. I felt very confident and Patel also said I was driving fine. On Sunday, I took the car to the highway and felt very comfortable. After driving on busy Indian roads, driving in the USA is much easier.

"Are you ready for a driving test with the DMV folks?" he asked. DMV is, Department of Motor Vehicles, which issues driving licenses.

"What are the expectations there?" I asked.

"The authority person will take you for a driving test followed by a multi-choice written test. If you qualify these two you will get the DL after biometric," he explained to me the process.

"I feel confident about the driving. I can practice reverse and parallel parking more today. But what about the test?" I asked.

"I will give you tips and you will pass the test," he laughed.

"What kind of tips?" I was perplexed.

"Please follow these thumb rules: (a) out of all true and false type of questions, always answer 'True'; (b) on multiple-choice questions always tick on the answer with a maximum number of characters," he explained the logic with ease and confidence.

I was shocked to hear his revelation.

'How can that be the case? I will anyways read the instructions and prepare well,' I thought as I was not sure about such tricks.

"Let us go there on Tuesday. I will take a half-day leave," I told him.

In DMV the inspector sat with me and asked me to follow a driving path. I drove confidently and completed all tasks as asked. He then prepared his report in the car itself and asked me to come for the written test. I started the written test and found questions quite easy. I was stuck in two questions and applied Patel's instructions and found that the logic was fine, I was really surprised. I passed the test and after biometric and photo, I got my USA Driving License shortly. I was excited to have achieved the next milestone in the USA journey.

Anita's flight reached Chicago, and I received her. Both of us were pretty excited. The next days and weeks were very exciting for me to show her around the city, malls, shopping for Sofa, shopping for groceries from Indian store, Jai Hind. But, I felt restricted in moving around. I had my DL and now it needed my first car in the US.

When you meet The Best Sales Person

I had shortlisted two brands Honda and Toyota. I had done some research that, the Japanese cars (primarily Honda and Toyota) are value for money as they run for long without giving any maintenance problem. Besides, the resale prices are good even after 5-6 years. I also had heard that Car Salespersons in the USA, are THE BEST SALES persons, and they pull all the tricks to 'nail you down' (try to close the deal) in the first meeting itself. I wanted to first look at both Honda Accord and Toyota Camry cars, take the test drive and then decide which car to buy. I decided to go alone to explore these two cars and take a test drive, and when I will finalize one out of the two cars, then I will take Anita to show the car to her and finalize the deal. I left the house with that plan and reached the Schaumburg Honda Automobile first as it was very close to my house.

"How can I help you?" salesperson, Mike, came and asked me.

"I am here to check out the new Honda Accord," I told him.

"Excellent choice. You have come to the right place," he responded.

"Let me clarify very clearly, that I am not going to buy it today. I am trying to compare between Honda Accord and Toyota Camry and after that only I will make my decision," I set the expectations.

"Don't worry, you will love the new Honda Accord," he was confident.

Since, I was aware of the sales tricks, I smiled and moved forward.

"This is a new Accord," he was friendly and explained the features.

"Let us go for a ride," he offered me the test drive with him.

I took the car out of the dealership and I drove around for a short trip. He kept on impressing me with different features of the car during the drive and then we came back. I loved the features and smooth ride.

"Ok, give me a deal so that when I take a test ride of Toyota Camry and then go back, I can compare everything to make a call," I told him.

He smiled and asked me to sit across a table.

"You know the car deal is already pasted on the car. But I will give you a special deal, I will get the corrosion and rust paint done for free and an extended warranty worth $500 for free," he offered me the deal.

"That's great, but what about any discount on the car?" I asked.

"If you make the down payment, I will give you another $500 off. But the offer is for today only." He offered.

"But I told you that I will not buy the car today," I reminded him.

"I understand but I am giving the special deal to beat my competition and if you go then this special deal will be off," he spoke.

"How are you planning to make the payment?" he further asked.

"I want to get it financed," I replied.

"I will give you the best deal if you buy it now. I will help you and give you a lower than the prevailing market finance rate that you can check out. I will get the finance approval done right now," he lured me further to buy the car now itself.

"But Mike, I have not taken a test drive of Toyota Camry and had told you that I will make take call after that only," I was stuck to my stand.

"Let me show you some studies that will help you in comparing the two cars you have shortlisted. You already have taken a test drive of the Honda Accord," he brought a different angle to satisfy my urge.

He shared some comparative studies where the two cars were almost at par but Honda Accord scored a little better on few points.

"You can see that both the cars are at par but Honda Accord has an edge feature-wise," he tried to satisfy my urge to compare.

"Cost-wise Accord is a little lower than Camry anyways. And today is the last day of the month and I need to complete my target and hence I am giving you all the special deals," he gave his reason for the deal.

"I appreciate your offer but then I had shared my intentions at the beginning itself. You are now pushing me," I said with a smile.

"SoDeep, all I am trying to do is to give you the best deal that no one else can give you," he tried to impress me with his genuine reason.

Most of the people in the USA pronounced my name as 'SoDeep' rather than 'Sudeep' and initially, I tried to correct some of them but then I accepted the way they pronounced it. I also felt that the meaning of 'SoDeep' is good in a way, so, whenever anyone used to face a problem in pronouncing my name, I used to break my name and ask them to call me 'So-Deep' which they understood easily.

The 'Accord' deal became very tempting for me now. I had checked the prices from a few sources and this sounded a great deal.

He saw me in little confused and found his moment of 'go for a kill' (a term used in aggressive sales technique, as I learned later).

"SoDeep, you are a nice guy. Let me give you my final deal that nobody can give you and which will help you make a decision right now. I tell you what, I will give you $250 further off. This is my final deal and if you take the car right now. I must tell you that since you are new to the USA, your credit history is not yet very strong which negatively impacts the financing and we never give such a deal in these cases but I will help you out with financing and this special deal," he tried to nail me.

I started laughing and he could see that I am almost in his trap.

"But I need my wife to finalize the deal," I told him smiling.

"No problem, let us go and get her right now. Your house is not far. Which color would you like?" he further offered and asked.

"What colors of car do you have?" I checked

"We have Frost White, Mystic Blue Pearl, and Eucalyptus Green Pearl. Take a look at them," he said quickly sensing the deal is almost done.

I liked Eucalyptus Green Pearl color but decided to call Anita.

"I am at Schaumburg Honda and the deal is almost finalized. Now we need to finalize the color. They have Frost White, Mystic Blue Pearl, and Eucalyptus Green Pearl. Which one?" After the update, I asked.

"What? But you had gone for the test drive and then wanted to decide tomorrow?" she was surprised.

"It's a long story and I will explain later, right now tell me which color would you like and I will bring that car to show you," I laughed.

"You decide but Eucalyptus Green Pearl sounds good," she replied.

"Eucalyptus Green Pearl, it is. Let us take it to my house because I surely want to show it to my wife first before finalizing," I told Mike.

We drove in Eucalyptus Green Pearl Honda Accord and reached my apartment complex. Anita saw the car and liked it very much.

"So, this is it. Let us go and complete the formalities," I told Mike.

I was nailed down by one of the notoriously famous American car sales guys, in a single meeting itself. He successfully sold me the car and that too, to my satisfaction.

I got the real-life experiential learning on:

"Aggressive yet Effective Sales with Customer Focus & Satisfaction"

Chapter 25

Life with a car became very good, and we started roaming around.

Deborah Brown was very happy with me, and my position became very credible in Sears Project. Around the October timeframe, my colleagues Sameer Munje and Sanjay Shanbagh also got placed in my project. By now the team size of Foundation consultants, in Sears, had grown significantly and the company was quite happy with this growth. This strengthened my position inside Foundation. In October 1997, I was rewarded by the CEO of Foundation, Sam Iyengar for:

"Dedication to work you have demonstrated in your present assignment at Sear, Chicago. In keeping with our motto, you went beyond the call of duty. This shows you are capable of consistent performance. We have also received strong feedback on the quality of your work from the client. This calls for special recognition". There was decent award money also along with the citation from the CEO. This gave my confidence a major boost. I realized that like in India if one focuses on work then, it's easy to be successful in the USA too.

Work-wise I was in a very good position as I had got new responsibilities, leading a few people technically, and I also started writing specifications along with the functional teams. I was further given a larger responsibility to work as a technical leader, along with, Judy Menezes, the functional leader of the 'Benefits module' of PeopleSoft. My dedication and contribution were paying. I was happy with this growth as I was learning more rapidly with a larger role. My hunger for learning and growth was getting the food of knowledge.

Big Learning in the USA was on, how to balance '**Excellence with Fun**'. Due to the working culture in the USA, everyone used to leave the office in time and no one used to call after office hours as it was considered unethical. This gave me a lot of time for fun with family and friends. Additionally, during summer, the days were long with sunset at around 8:30-9 PM giving a lot of day time for family and friends. I could see Anita being very happy about this. She was getting much more time and attention from me in the USA than in India.

Many of my ex-Raymond colleagues had moved to the USA by now. We all decided to have a get-together during Christmas at my home. Ravi Ghantasala, Surendra Kamath, Rupa Gadgil, Himanshu Gadgil, and Samir Joshi flew from various parts of the USA and came to stay with us. Mahesh Kambli was in Chicago with his family. We visited various places in Chicago in Christmas snow including Sears Towers.

PK had taken immigration to Canada and had joined BAAN, another big ERP of the time. He was based in Toronto. When he heard about the get-together of ex-Raymond colleagues, at my house during Christmas time, he also drove down from Toronto to Chicago. He arrived a couple of days before the new year. It was a big fun fiesta.

Everything was on track for me. I was getting recognized by customers (Sears), employers (Foundation), and my colleagues. My position was becoming better and better from my growth perspective– officially, socially, and financially. My aggression and hurt were going down. It was almost a year being in the USA so we decided to visit India during the Holi festival in 1998. I took five weeks' leave to visit India. We were excited for our first India trip after coming to the USA. We did a lot of shopping for everyone, especially for my nieces and nephews.

We took an Air India flight from Chicago to New Delhi via London. It was a delight to see the family members. Family is family.

I could see the difference in how we were getting treated by society this time. My status was now linked to my being in the USA and doing well in the IT industry. I thought, my retaliation is going in the right direction. I have achieved decent success, though not enough.

I had two purposes for this visit. Firstly, to see my loved ones and the well-wishers as I was missing them. They helped me in my days of rejection and misery which I can never forget. Secondly, I wanted to see the reaction in the eyes of those who had ruled me off.

But my anger had subsided against my detractors. I was more interested to enjoy my good times with my loved ones. I met all my loved ones on this trip and had a fantastic time. I always have loved the kids of my sisters and brother, more than anything, so I had called all of them, Prakhar, Aastha, Saakshi, Tejas, and Srijan to my parent's home so that we can have maximum fun together. I could see pure love for me in their eyes and I felt nothing in life is more important than this love. They started accepting me now since I was doing well.

For a moment, I thought of visiting Kalpana's father and sharing my success. The thoughts came to my mind "What if the future could have been seen?" "Could, I have been rejected by her even then?" "What will her mother think of me now?" But then different thoughts came to my mind, "What is the use of all this now?" "What will change now?" "What will I gain from this?" "Am I missing anything now?" "Am I trying to make people jealous or regret?" With a calm mind when I thought about these questions, I realized that I honestly did not blame anyone as it was more of circumstances. Besides, I did not want to make anyone uncomfortable. My personal life is going great and I do not want to carry any regret or hatred. I decided not to meet him.

Vivek was indeed right, "society will not change, and if you are sensitive and have to live with them, then you must take appropriate actions so that they do not reject you."

On this trip, I could see that 'The Society' had changed its views and this made me realize that **"I am not a rejected or outcasted anymore."** Trip was very rejuvenating and we came back reenergized.

In Foundation Software, my annual performance appraisal went very well and my work in Sears was recognized and highly appreciated. Feedback given by Deborah Brown on my performance did following:

- Increased positioning of Foundation consultants in Sears project.
- Increased consultants from Foundation in Sears within one year.
- Increased Foundation revenues from Sears account.
- Enhanced my positioning—Awarded by the Foundation CEO.
- I was all set to get higher salary raise.

I was surprised to receive multiple job calls and offers from the US market though, I had not applied anywhere. I knew that PeopleSoft is a niche technology and in high demand and hence there are a lot of opportunities. However, I was surprised to see how these companies are getting my personal information even my current compensation structure as well. I suspected that such information can only be shared by, ex-employees or current employees but I was not sure. Recruiters hunted for all such resources using their skills and network.

The offers were very lucrative with a huge salary hike and though I was happy with my current positioning, project, and salary yet there was temptation. I remembered the earlier learning that, one has to keep an eye on the opportunities around, and shall not reject an opportunity without looking at it or knowing about it.

Chapter 26

The offer from RPM systems was very lucrative, with a huge raise in salary and additional benefits and placement in Toyota Motor Manufacturing, the largest car manufacturing plants in the USA.

"Take the offer, as this will give you major learning and growth, which was your prime objective of coming to the USA. All these organizations are doing business and making money. They do not think twice to fire a person if they don't have an opportunity for them. So do not think emotionally and instead think practically about your growth first," **I got The Advice from a senior PeopleSoft professional.**

This advice helped me make up my mind. I realized that I have helped Foundation for a year to grow the account so I have given my due to the organization and now I must think about my basic objective of coming to the US. I tendered my resignation, giving proper notice.

"Oh God, where is this plane landing. Is there a problem?" I thought with worry as the plane seemed to be landing in the large grass fields. I saw horses running in the grass fields very close to the plane.

I had accepted the RPM systems offer and had joined them. I have taken a flight from Chicago O'Hare airport to Blue Grass Airport, Lexington, Kentucky as I was going to report at the Toyota project.

I saw, no one else was worried or reacting like I was.

"Is the airfield in between the grass fields?" I started thinking. And then the plane landed safely on the runway. I took a huge sigh of relief.

Kentucky is a south-eastern state bounded by the Ohio River in the north and the Appalachian Mountains in the east, with Frankfort the state capital. The state is home to the Kentucky Derby, the renowned horse race as well world-famous Kentucky Fried Chicken (KFC).

Lexington is a city in Kentucky. It's known for horse farms and thoroughbred racetracks like Keeneland. Known as the "Horse Capital of the World", it is the heart of the state's Bluegrass region.

"Hi, I am Dee Greene, and I am the project manager of the PeopleSoft HRMS project. You will be working with me on the project as a senior PeopleSoft analyst," the project manager introduced herself to me after I met her and shared my introduction.

"Pleasure meeting you, Dee. I am looking forward to working with you on the project," I responded courteously.

"Let me get going with your induction activities," she said with a smile.

"That will be great," I nodded and smiled back.

I was taken to see the Toyota Motor Manufacturing Plant.

Toyota Motor Manufacturing plant in Georgetown, Kentucky, is Toyota's largest vehicle manufacturing plant in the world, spreading across 1300+ acres and a total facility size of 8.1 million sq. ft., equal to 169 football fields under one roof, with 8000+ full-time employees. The plant can produce 550,000 vehicles and 600,000+ engines annually. This is the world's only manufacturing facility where three different segments of cars (premium sedan, SUV, and Luxury) were manufactured on a single assembly line. It builds the bestselling premium sedan car in the USA, Toyota Camry, Toyota Avalon, and Luxury car Lexus. The plant starts the operation by taking simple flat iron sheets and then performs all kinds of operations like stamping, die, manufacturing, body weld, paint, plastics, vehicle assembly, engine machining, and assembly to produce a finished ready car.

The plant was so big that I was taken on a travel cart and was shown the complete car manufacturing process, starting from, flat iron sheets getting picked and taken to the assembly line where it is moulded and various parts of the car get added, one by one, and then to a part of the assembly line called 'marriage section' where the engine comes from another line and gets added into the car (like adding the heart to a body), and then to the paint section, and finally rolling out the finished car. It was a mind-blowing and overwhelming experience to see the magnitude and scale, of the complete operation, and the kind of giant robotic sections at various locations.

"How minuscule we are and what we do." I thought after seeing this.

Thereafter, I was taken to a hall of fame where I was presented with the famous book 'Toyota Way' by one of the senior officials of Toyota. He advised me to read the book and I humbly agreed.

The next day, I was introduced to the project team and was given a brief about the project and my work. The work environment was very unique, and very unlike where ever I had worked. There was a huge hall with similar desks all over the floor. I was told that all employees of the information technology department sit here no matter how senior or junior that person is. So, no differentiation of position to the workspace. I was so impressed with this concept of equality among all.

I started the work, and quickly, I made my impression on Dee Greene. Funny thing was that in the Toyota project also, the time allocated for the work assigned to me was much more than what I needed, so, I finished the assigned work very quickly.

Like Deborah in Sears, here also, initially Dee Greene looked at me with surprise and doubt, but when found my work to be perfect, she also was very happy with my performance and had started depending on me very quickly. In this project, I was also doing customer support work in addition to the development work. This gave me very good exposure to, the typical behaviour of an end customer in the US. I learned the tricks and keywords, important for customer satisfaction.

I found a nice 1BHK apartment in Lexington. One side drive from the apartment to the office was of approximately 30 minutes. Unlike in Chicago, there were very few Indians in Lexington. Luckily in Raintree Apartment Homes, there were three Indian families, Anil & Shalini Sharma, Bharat & Ila Shah, and Anurag & Shilpa Shroff. Bharat also was working in Toyota as a contractor, through a different company. We all jelled so well in very little time, and became like a family. We visited many places of natural beauty nearby like: Natural bridge: Natural sandstone arch, formed in millions of years; Mammoth Cave: World's longest known cave system, with more than 400 miles explored, and one of the oldest tourist attractions; Kentucky Derby: This is one of the most famous horse racecourses; Cumberland Falls: Also called Mini Niagara Falls.

I had a colleague named Sarah. Once, I invited her home and introduced her to Anita. We sat with some snacks, drinks.

"How many kids do you have?" Sarah asked Anita curiously.

"We do not have any yet," Anita responded shyly.

"How many kids do you have?" Anita now asked Sarah.

"Let me see. Well, I have a boy and a girl from my current husband. I also have two from my first husband. And my husband has one from his previous marriage. So, we have five kids." She started with a thinking mode and then calculation mode and then finally responded.

I could see Anita's face completely dazed with this and the way Sarah answered. This may be a common thing in the US but not India.

One day, in the office, I was talking to a colleague and he said "This weekend, I have taken an appointment with my parents, and I am looking forward to meeting them." This again was a new for me as I had not heard of taking an appointment with parents to meet them.

In the Toyota project, I became very close to the HR department users, and being curious, I understood their challenges and started giving solutions, going out of the way. I learned one of the challenges.

Toyota encouraged perfect attendance from all of its employees. They launched 'Perfect Attendance Awards' to encourage and reward employees with perfect attendance every year. As a process, all employees with perfect attendance in a year were identified and shortlisted. Then a draw of 20 employees, from the shortlisted employees, were taken out. Each of these 20 employees was awarded a brand-new Toyota Camry car. The pain for the HR department was that all this was a manual process. I offered to automate all this in a new application "The perfect Attendance Award System", to be built within the PeopleSoft HRMS application. I built the application in a very short period and handed it over to the HR team. Dee Greene and the HR team were very happy. **I learned that taking initiative is very important**. I started more improvement opportunities with the HR team, which gave me an understanding of how Toyota adopts Kaizen.

Kaizen is a Japanese term meaning "change for the better" or "continuous improvement." It is a Japanese business philosophy regarding the processes that continuously improve operations and involve all employees. By improving standardized programs and processes, kaizen aims to eliminate waste and redundancies (lean manufacturing). Kaizen was first practiced in Japanese businesses after World War II, influenced in part by American business and quality-management teachers, and most notably as part of The Toyota Way. It has since spread throughout the world and has been applied to environments outside business and productivity. Two kaizen approaches have been distinguished, Point Kaizen (happens quickly and without much planning by fixing the problem instantly.) and System Kaizen (accomplished in an organized manner and is devised to address system-level problems in an organization.)

With my understanding of the theory of Kaizen, when I visited the manufacturing floors to see how Kaizen works in real life. I was given the live example: when a worker on a conveyer belt, tries to attach the car door then the person can suggest improvements as to where the car door will be kept, or where the tools are, and what will be the more convenient and time-saving thing, for that worker to fix the door. If any suggestion from him reduces car door fixing time, then the whole improvement saves time as well as adds convenience for the worker. This is one such example of Kaizen. Since, workers on the ground face challenges on a day-to-day basis, the possibility of an improvement coming from them is much practical. This is why in Kaizen, all employees are involved, related to that process. One can learn a lot from the Japanese way of working and so did I.

It was very odd for me to drive to the Toyota plant in my Honda Accord, whereas almost all workers were driving their Toyota Cars.

Dee Greene, project manager, and my reporting manager gave me fantastic appreciation letter for: 'Recognizing hard work', 'Being a valuable asset to Toyota', 'Always ensuring meeting deadlines', ''Always gone beyond what is expected of you, 'Relied on you and you have never let me down', 'You constantly amaze me with your solutions and being very intelligent, clever and resourceful which is the feeling of every user worked with you', 'Appreciate you guiding team members' and 'It would have been very hard to find someone else that could have come in and made the difference that you have in the time that you have been here.' This was a huge moment of pride for me that boosted my morale, passion, and positivity to do more. Appreciation indicated that my quest is going in the right direction.

Mike Becker, joined as the Director of PeopleSoft Services in RPM Systems. He called me to understand the Toyota project. Very soon, he informed me that he wants to start a PeopleSoft practice across the company. He was based in Cincinnati, Ohio, which was around 1.5 hours driving distance from my home. I reached there and had a brainstorming session on creating the PeopleSoft practice. We created a structure around it. There were various parts of the practice including hiring, training, central support for all PeopleSoft consultants. I saw this as a huge opportunity to learn and happily got involved in the practice creation as it was giving me much larger exposure. I got engaged in major activities like practice support, presales, and centralized hiring.

"Sudeep, you need to help in one of the sales bids as a presale person in the Detroit area," the regional sales head Darren called me for help.

"Sure. I would love to," I happily agreed as this was good exposure.

We went to Detroit and met the prospect. During the sales pitch, I started giving real-time examples– how various processes and issues are handled in the industry and how have we handled them. The prospect team got very much curious and went into the details, which was a good sign from a sales perspective, as this shows that the prospect is interested. During such sales cycles, I realized that the customers want to hear the real experience, rather than pure sale talk. I was very glad that the pitch went very well and I got the exposure and confidence to handle the sales bid as an SME (subject matter expert). All the PeopleSoft hiring interviews started passing through me. I used to take the final interview and decide if the person is the right fit for PeopleSoft practice or not. This gave me a lot of exposure to the current skill levels in the industry. I became more critical of the company.

Our company name was changed from RPM Systems to Rapidigm.

A close friend lost his mother in India and he could not see her body, as, by the time he took the earliest possible flight and reached India, the body had to be cremated. I saw him cry and that made a huge impact on my mind. I decided to return after completing 5 years.

"Sudeep, we have got a very important project for you in the Boston area. We have pitched you as the Technical Project Lead and Application Architect," Mike Becker called me and informed me.

"Ok Mike, what is the project about?" I asked.

"This is for one of the most niche educational institutions and they want to implement PeopleSoft HRMS application," he shared.

"I would love to join a fresh implementation project as here it is more of a support along with some development," I shared my interest.

"Ok then, Boston area sales folks will get in touch with you," he said.

With over a year each in Sears Project in Chicago and Toyota Project in Lexington, it was time for us to move to the Boston area to work with a customer called College of the Holy Cross, a highly reputed college. We also felt happy as we were moving back to a bigger metro town.

- Toyota project gave me immense learning:
    - Learned Toyota Way of working
    - Lean Manufacturing;
    - Focus on long term goals;
    - Listening is very important to learn;
    - Continuous improvement is critical;
    - Add value by challenging yourself and doing better;
    - Importance of communication to improve & maintain process;
- Learned Kaizen and saw how it is implemented on the ground.
- Importance of taking initiatives by observing needs—gives rewards.
- Customer interaction is critical to understand their mindset.
- Perseverance with Passion, Patience, and Positivity brings Pride.
- How PeopleSoft practice works and what are its components.
- Importance of presales; Prospects want to hear real experience.
- Importance of the centralized hiring process– right fit consultant.

Chapter 27

"Sudeep is one of the best PeopleSoft consultants in the industry. His contributions to the Sears Roebuck and Toyota Motor Manufacturing projects have been highly applauded by the customers. Toyota wanted to continue with his support but looking at the gravity and importance of this project, we have requested his services for this project." Darren, the sales director of Rapidigm, introduced me to William Conley, the HR Director of the College of the Holy Cross.

Earlier, I had left Lexington and had reached Worcester, a suburb of Boston, to join the PeopleSoft HRMS project at the College of the Holy Cross. I was projected as a larger than life professional at Holy Cross by our sales team. If asked, whether I am the best PeopleSoft consultant, I would have not agreed. I would rather have said that "I have given my best and got good feedback from customers and that's all about me." But **I learned that in sales, one thing works 'Jo dikhta hai, ya dikhaya jata hai, wo hi bikta hai (What is visible, or made visibly, gets sold)' so they paint such an image that it gets sold.**

The city of Boston is the capital of Massachusetts state in the USA. The city is the economic and cultural anchor of a substantially larger metropolitan area known as the Greater Boston, home to a census-estimated 4.8 million people. Boston is one of the oldest municipalities in the USA and today is a thriving centre of scientific research. The Boston area's many colleges and universities make it a world leader in higher education, including law, medicine, engineering, and business. The city is considered to be a global pioneer in entrepreneurship & innovation, with nearly 5,000 start-ups.

Worcester, also established by the early British settlers, is approximately 40 miles west of Boston and is named after Worcester in England. In the 1990s, education, medicine, biotechnology, and new immigrants started to make their mark in the city. My assignment was to help higher education from an information technology perspective.

The **College of the Holy Cross** is a private liberal arts college in Worcester, a suburb of Boston, in Massachusetts. Founded in 1843, Holy Cross is a highly reputed college, part of the NEASC (New England Association of Schools and Colleges). Described as one of the Hidden Ivies for academics, its alumni include Supreme Court Judge, State Governor, Senator, Chairman, CEO, President of Federal Reserve Bank, Actors, Pulitzer Prize-winning authors, Entrepreneurs, and Nobel Laureates. The college premise was spread over a big hillock. It is one of the most advanced colleges, in terms of adopting technology.

I was briefed about the adoption of the PeopleSoft Application to automate and integrate processes of HRMS and Campus solutions. All the major modules of PeopleSoft— HR, Benefits, Payroll were to be implemented. Rapidigm was awarded the project to implement PeopleSoft HRMS as implementation partners of Holy Cross. The team was formed to implement PeopleSoft HRMS with eight consultants from Rapidigm and around four from Holy Cross. The team members were from the United States, Canada, England, France, Mexico, China, and India. Such a unique form of the team was very interesting. Team members were Ian Wood, Joyce McCauley, Nick Yurchuck, Julie Collins, Nancy Pfafflein, Linda Kou, Madeline, and me. Later, Raghav Pujari and Sampath Muniyapalli, Saravanan, and Audrey also joined the project. Team diversity was a challenge as well as learning.

Department of Human Resources at the College of Holy Cross was headed by William Conley (an ex-navy seal), supported by leaders like Pat Morrissett, Donna Wrenn, among others. In my initial interactions, I found them very knowledgeable, focused, approachable, and kind.

The project plan was created and the work started, including the understanding of the current processes (As-Is system), the gaps (Pain Points), and the expectations from the new system (To-Be System). These were rigorous sessions with the HR team, and I quickly found that the expectations are quite advanced. I had not seen such a level of automation in many big organizations and was very impressed. I knew this project will give me immense learning and fulfilment.

I found our new residence in Princeton Place Apartments on 285 Plantation Street in Worcester near UMass Memorial Medical Centre and Lake Quinsigamond. It was a nice 1BHK apartment. The Greater Boston area and Worcester also had a lot of Indians. We made good friends quickly with Rajesh-Uma, Srini-Vanaja, Ravi-Geetha besides a few others. My Foundation colleague, Venu Iyer, also was in Boston.

On the work front, we started requirement gathering to understand the current processes, the pain points, and the need. In parallel, this project needed to convert the historical data from legacy applications to PeopleSoft applications. As the technical lead, I was responsible for this. Though PeopleSoft provides a data conversion script yet there were a lot of loopholes. I asked for help from various sources but did not get any help. I took things in a war mode and decided to understand the complete thing myself, including the architecture table structure of the complete application, and then create my data conversion scripts. **This was the only option left for me but was a humongous challenge.**

I started studying the complex architecture of PeopleSoft database tables. But ERP companies do not provide all the details of the design to protect their Intellectual Proprietary. This meant that there are hidden details that I needed to understand. I evolved an approach. I created a few utilities to check the logic and details of the data flow, in the tables, based on the online data entry. I followed the data entry steps and ran the utilities after each step. This approach gave me in-depth knowledge of all the functionality and the corresponding technical handling of the code. By the end of this exercise, I had in-depth knowledge of the complete PeopleSoft HRMS application – functional, technical, and architecture.

Though before joining this project, I had fantastic technical and functional knowledge of the PeopleSoft application and was highly appreciated by Sears and Toyota teams, yet with this in-depth exercise, I was able to visualize the process flow and information flow in detail. So now, in the requirement sessions, I used to know exactly what needs to be done. As a result, besides being the technical lead, I also started helping functional teams, whenever they faced any issue. This impressed my functional colleagues in Rapidigm as well as Holy Cross leaders, including Bill, Pat, and Donna.

Learning: Rich knowledge & Confidence comes after taking a tough hands-on approach with Passion, Perseverance and Patience.

"I think I have learned well. I can be called a subject matter expert now," I felt fulfilled and happy with my achievement. 'The Rebel' in me, mellowed down further, and my original 'Happy Soul' emerged back. Work Excellence was on the right track. I thought that I need to give more attention to the fun quotient now.

I had seen RV (Recreation Vehicle) advertisements on TV and heard fantastic reviews of an RV camping trip from friends and was told that this is a 'Must Do' activity. We planned a camping trip to the White Mountains in New Hampshire in an RV along with friends and it was fun. We also went to the Grand Canyon and Las Vegas trip and decided to drive there using Arizona deserted highways shown in many movies. We took a helicopter ride to see the Grand Canyon and spent quality time in Las Vegas. It was just larger than life experience.

I came to the USA to establish myself as materialistically acceptable. Now, I had a feeling of fulfilment on the work and home front. We already had spent almost three years in the USA. We decided that we need to start making plans to go back to India, after completing five years. We also were facing tremendous pressure, from both our families, to go for a baby now. I wanted to first establish myself professionally, so, I had resisted for a baby. But now, with some success on that front, both of us were feeling ready for the new phase of life and starting a family with a baby.

At Holy Cross, the project was going in full swing now and implementation was in the advanced stage. I had become very close to Bill and Pat and was putting my heart and soul to give them the best experience of implementation. I went out of the way to suggest more best practices. This was well appreciated by Holy Cross leaders.

We were on cloud nine when we heard that Anita is pregnant.

"Here is the baby. Do you want to know if it's a boy or girl?" the lady doing the ultrasound showed the baby and asked us.

"No, not now," we said as we had decided to keep it a surprise.

"Are you sure?" She said smiling looking at the baby on the screen.

We got a little curious and tempted at her looks, while she was looking at the baby. We did not say anything.

"Are you sure you don't want to know?" she asked now looking at us.

"Ok, tell us then," I said abruptly with a little curiosity. I got lured.

"Congratulation honey, you are having a baby boy," she announced.

"Congratulations. Due date is 23rd January," Dr. Jane Molinari told us.

We are going to have a Baby Boy.

Chapter 28

Three factors in mind were influencing me to return to India:

- I felt I have accomplished my purpose of coming to the US as I had learned and achieved success, more than I had ever thought.
- I still remember the incident when my friend's mother had died and he could not reach in time for her last rights and felt guilty.
- We are going to be parents. I had seen many friends who could not return to India as their kids did not want to move. We thought he can decide his move after getting a good education in India.

We decided to go back to India by the end of 2001, after completing five years in the US, around 1.5 years from now. I decided to give advance intimation about my plans, to Rapidigm and Holy Cross. I was very close to Bill (William Conley) and Pat, I decided to inform them first as they were having long-term plans for me as they had told me.

"We are going to have a baby around January 20th," I Informed Bill.

"That is fantastic news. Congratulations," he sounded very happy.

"I also wanted to tell you that we are planning to move back to India after around 1.5 years from now to settle back there," I revealed.

"That is not good news for us. Why do you want to move?" Bill asked.

"My parents are getting old and I want to be with them," I told him.

"That is so sweet. They are lucky to have a son like you," he spoke.

"Thanks, but actually, I want them more than they want me. My brother and sisters are there to take care of them, but I don't want to miss them in their old age," I further clarified emotionally.

"I understand," Bill said and patted my back.

The next day Bill called me and gave me an advice cum offer.

"Now that you have decided to go back in 1.5 years, I want you to join Holy Cross as an employee. That way we will be sure that you will remain with us during your remaining period, and not be deployed elsewhere by Rapidigm. This will be good for you as you can stay in one location with your young kid. We will give you a good salary increase. Right now, we pay an hourly rate which is very high and even if we pay you an increased salary, we still end up saving money. While, in Holy Cross, this will be a very high salary than what we offer to our employees. But this will be fine since your appointment will be for only a short term since you will go back to India after 1.5-2 years," he shared his fantastic, well-thought-through win-win-win plan.

"Sounds like a good plan. I will be okay if Rapidigm is okay," I told him.

"Sure, since you are ok I will talk to them," he said.

I thought, that Rapidigm will not be okay as they will lose billing.

"Do you want to join Holy Cross?" Rapidigm regional head asked me.

"That will be good and stable for me during this time," I explained.

Rapidigm and Holy Cross discussed the plan and agreed for me to join Holy Cross with condition that Holy Cross will pay a transfer fee to Rapidigm as well as put a replacement consultant in my place.

The deal was agreed between Rapidigm & Holy Cross. I also agreed.

Mike Becker was not happy with this as apparently, Rapidigm regional team did not take him in confidence. I thought he must have been consulted and that's how Rapidigm has agreed. Big misunderstanding.

Since Mike was a very good Boss, and I was close to him, I called him and explained to him about the misunderstanding and then explained to him about Anita's pregnancy and the plan to move back to India in max 1.5 years. He understood my perspective of stability in one place.

After all the confusion was resolved, I was called by Bill.

"Here is your offer as discussed. Please look at it," he gave the offer.

"Thanks, Bill, for your initiative and consideration," I responded.

"Well, look at it and let me know if you have any questions," he spoke.

I opened the envelope and was delighted to see the offer. In addition, they offered me an independent fully furnished, and fully serviced, company-owned house to live in without any charges. This in itself was a worth huge amount. I was happily surprised and delighted.

"Thank you so much, Bill," I thanked him from the core of my heart.

Bill had given me an amazing deal and at the same time, he saved huge money for the Holy Cross, besides securing the stability of the project through me. He also gave a good commission to Rapidigm.

Learning: This was a true win-win-win deal that Bill had orchestrated. I was amazed and learned the true tricks of making a deal. One can be creative and make similar win-win-win deals by taking care of the interests of all the parties involved.

This indeed was a super achievement and I was overwhelmed.

"I have got some good advice which has helped me in **sailing through the curves of my life**. I can never express my gratitude in words to these angels in life. There is no need to be a **Rebel** anymore and continue with this **Retaliation**," I concluded.

I joined the College of the Holy Cross as an 'Applications Architect' and was also given the responsibility to manage the PeopleSoft project and some other programs.

I shifted to the new house, provided by the College of the Holy Cross. This was located on top of a hillock, on the boundary of Holy Cross premise, and was within a walking distance from my office building. This was a big three-story fully furnished independent house. The ground floor had a walk-in room, a drawing room with all the furniture, a kitchen with all the amenities and utensils, a furnished dining room, and a study room. The first floor had two fully furnished bedrooms and an attic room. The basement had utilities like the heating plant with boilers, washing machine, dryer, etc. There was a separate garage building inside the property. The house was surrounded by a big open backyard, front and side lawns with many big trees, and a variety of flower plants. The house was on an uphill road ending on the boundary of the

College of the Holy Cross. There were around 20 houses on the road, around 10 on each side. We were the only Indians living among the population of native Americans. We shifted and settled with our stuff.

"Dhoom! Dhoom!" Around 1 PM in the night we heard a huge noise from downstairs. We got up and looked at each other worried.

"Did you hear that sound?" we asked each other and nodded. We tried to concentrate and hear what is going on downstairs. There was silence for the next few minutes. We laid down but did not sleep.

"Dhoom! Dhoom!" the noise came again as if someone is breaking in.

"God, someone is downstairs," Anita whispered in my ears.

"Let us be very quiet and try to listen," I whispered in her ears.

It was quiet for some time and then again, a similar noise came. This time I looked at my bedroom door and noticed that there was no door lock or latches. By now the atmosphere was very tense and I also was worried thinking it may be a break-in. The house was full of glass windows on the ground floor and anybody could have easily broken in with a slight punch on the glass windows since there were no grills. I considered calling the police but decided to wait. There was a rod in the room so I took that quietly and stood behind the door trying to hear if someone is coming upstairs. After a while, the noises stopped. We thought someone may have heard my footsteps on the first floor and hence may be sitting silent. We also kept on waiting silently trying to listen to any movement or noise. But we did not hear anything.

Around 5:30 AM when we saw the daylight, I decided to go down and see what has happened. When we went down, neither did we find anyone, not anything missing. We were very surprised. We suspected someone may have broken in through the keys and may have left after hearing our movement on the first floor.

I initially thought to report this to Holy Cross but then out of hesitation, I decided not to do so. We went to Walmart and purchased locks and latches for doors and installed them. In the night we waited for some time then went to sleep.

"Dhoom! Dhoom!" we heard the sound again in the night as we were about to sleep. I looked at our door and was a little less worried seeing the door lock and the additional latches.

I again took the rod in hand and stayed in the room. The noise came a few times and then it stopped again. I was perplexed but did not want to go down. In the morning, I went downstairs and did not find anything missing. This was very surprising.

The next night again the sound came and I decided to go down. There was no one on the ground floor. I waited for a few moments and heard that the noise was coming from the basement. I thought either someone has broken in through a small ventilation window in the basement that opens on the garage side or something else. We had seen haunted movies where the basement is haunted. The next day morning, I went down to the basement and found that the ventilation window was intact and locked from inside which was very surprising for us. The incident repeated for a few more days and we were worried thinking if this is a haunted place. We decided to move back to the apartment and I thought I will talk to Bill about this. One of the maintenance guys came to our house and I shared this with him. He said that such sound comes from the boiler in the basement which generally starts in the night to maintain the heating in the house. Next night we actually saw that. We felt so foolish. We had a good laugh.

In Holy Cross, I had a meeting with the leaders and assessed the work priorities. We went live successfully and started helping users to adopt the PeopleSoft application. Soon application was smooth.

I met leaders and identified two priorities projects – Faculty Management System and the advanced One Card System integration with PeopleSoft HRMS. I discussed in detail the faculty management system with Ellen Keohane, associate director of the College. I created a plan and took agreement from the stakeholders.

Anita and I knew that we will not be able to travel after a couple of months, due to advanced pregnancy, and post that we will have to move back to India. So, we decided to take one more trip. We planned a trip to Los Angles, Hollywood, Universal Studios, and Disneyland. We reached Los Angles and took a tour of all the main attractions like Hollywood, Walk of Fame, Santa Monica, Beverly Hills, Universal Studios, and then we spent one whole day in Disney Land.

After we came back, rejuvenated, I started work in parallel on One Card System integration as well as the Faculty Management System. Integration of One Card was a relatively easier task whereas developing a new module of Faculty Management System, within PeopleSoft application, was a complete exercise. I started my work with a sense of urgency keeping timelines in mind.

Chapter 29

Dr. Jane Molinari was the **Obstetrician and Gynaecologist** and was looking after Anita for the growth of the baby. It was heartening to have discussions and understand the details of the growth of the baby in our monthly appointments. We found that there are websites where one can register with basic details of pregnancy and the website, in turn, sends a weekly standard growth status. The weekly update and best practice suggestions were very useful for us and we keenly started monitoring the growth of the baby and taking all steps.

With my detailed involvement, I started appreciating what and how much a female goes through during the pregnancy. This further increased my respect for their tolerance, sacrifices, and patience.

I decided that I will try to contribute everything in my control and capacity that is needed in this duration. I will play my part to the best.

I had planned to call a family member towards the advanced stage of pregnancy so that they can stay for some duration post-delivery as well. I asked the family to plan accordingly. Unfortunately, my parents as well as Anita's parents could not come due to the health issues of my father and Anita's father. I had high hopes from my favorite Shobha aunty. Unfortunately, her visa was rejected as well. There was no hope now for anyone to come to support us.

I don't know how, but I suddenly felt very strong and in control.

"This is so disappointing," Anita sounded very low.

"*Mai hi hu mata, pita mai hi hu, mai hi hu bandhu, sakha mai hi hu* (meaning now I will play all roles that of a father, mother, sibling, and friend). Please do not worry, I will do everything for you and will not let you feel the void," I told Anita in a mode of strength and positivity.

She smiled and loved what I told her. She also got positive and we decided to take control and manage it ourselves. I started decorating one bedroom for the baby. There are many beautiful baby specialty stores in the US, where one can buy all the baby items. These stores keep the items with the blue and pink theme. Blue for baby boy and pink for baby girl. We realized the importance of knowing the gender of the baby so that one can buy accordingly. We did a lot of shopping and decorated the room with a blue theme for our son. We joined LAMAZE classes where participants are taught relaxation techniques and breathing exercises to help ease the discomfort of labor and birth.

By now I had a fantastic friend circle in the USA and most of my friends had become like a family. When they came to know about no one can come from India to support us they stood by us and offered their support whenever and wherever needed.

One day, I was talking to my mother and she expressed her disappointment that she is not able to do 'God Bharai' (baby shower). I realized the importance of the ceremony and decided to organize it myself. I called a few of my friends in the US and within a few hours, we made the plan and finalized the date for the baby shower. It was decided that we will give Anita a surprise. Friends decided to travel from across the US and local friends pitched in as well. On the planned day of the baby shower, I dropped Anita at a friend's house in the morning (which was usual), saying I will pick her in the evening after the office. She did not suspect anything and happily went to the friend's place. During the day my friends arrived and they started decorating the house. Multiple varieties of food were prepared. It was a grand preparation. By evening, when we were all ready, I left to pick Anita and came back with her while friends were in the house. They had turned off the lights. The moment Anita entered the house everyone shouted "Surprise!!!" Anita was overwhelmed with the sudden surprise. I was happy that she did not miss this ceremony.

"You have pre-eclampsia, and that is why your blood pressure is very high. You need to strictly rest and lie down flat in the bed," Dr. Jane Molinari informed us when we visited to see her. Anita had told her about the headache and other symptoms. She was asked to take complete bed rest. The situation was very critical. I decided to take complete control of the situation. I needed to arrange for food as well as all other day-to-day needs which Anita was taking care of. I decided to spend time at home and talked to Bill about it. The leaders in Holy Cross were very considerate. When they knew about the situation, they asked me to work from home. I was called only if there is a critical need or a critical meeting. I could walk to the office on short notice. This was a big help for me in managing my home-related work.

I never had liked cooking. But now with Anita's condition, I needed to arrange the food. I found one Gujrati family which supplied Indian food but did not like the taste of the food. I decided to learn and cook. Anita told me the steps resting in her bed and I followed the steps in the kitchen downstairs. In a few days, I did learn to prepare basic food. I increased the quantum of fruit juices and dairy products in our food habits. Soon, I became quite good at managing quality food for both of us. My mom was very happy to hear about my cooking.

"I wish you both were in India. I would have prepared Dry Fruit Laddus for Anita," one day my mother told me over the phone.

I realized and decided to make dry fruit laddus and surprise Anita. I went to the Indian grocery store and bought cashew, almonds, nuts and quietly made around 80 dry fruit laddus. Then, I showed the laddus to Anita and she became very emotional.

"Mom, I made 80 Dry Fruit Laddus yesterday," I proudly called mom.

"What? This is good. Where did you get edible gum?' she was curious.

"What is edible gum?" I was surprised and asked.

"Oh, that gives warmth to the body. But do not worry, dry fruit laddus without it is also good. I am so proud of you," she said proudly.

The same day, I went to the Indian grocery store and got edible gum and more dry fruits and quietly prepared around 75 more dry fruit laddus but with edible gum. Anita was super overwhelmed. I felt proud. I hated cooking but this was a different situation. Females do so much for family and I felt this is the least I can do.

"Anita's father has to undergo heart surgery as his arteries are blocked," I was informed by my brother, Dhirendra.

"What? When? How? Where?" I asked so many questions in shock.

"His arteries are blocked and Doctors at Escorts hospital have advised an urgent surgery. Dr. Naresh Trehan is seeing the case. The surgery will be performed in a couple of days. Do not tell this to Anita as her BP is already very high and, in this condition, there will be an adverse impact on her and the baby. Let the operation be performed successfully and let Anita's condition improve and then you can tell her. This is what her parents want," he informed and advised me.

"Oh God, what kind of test is this? I will fight it out" I was worried, but I had no option but to be strong for the family, I reminded myself.

The operation was successful and after that, I informed Anita about it.

Chapter 30

The angel in life

White paratroopers started falling like cotton candy. The direction of their fall from the sky was random. The number of paratroopers, falling from the sky, increased gradually. And with that, the direction of their fall started moving in a slanted direction, not vertically down. I was watching this with amazement. Some of them fell on the trees and some were falling on the ground. New Year's Eve was approaching and with that, the dance of the wind had increased, as if there was a rush to cross the new year line. Suddenly, more and more paratroopers started falling but were getting blown a little horizontally by the raging wind. This was an amazing and awestruck view. The paratroopers were piling up on the trees, plants, grass, buildings, and roads. Snowflakes falling from the sky felt like white paratroopers coming down like cotton candy and dancing with the wind. It had snowed heavily for the past few days and the front and backyard of the house was covered with 2-4 feet of snow. Tree branches were bent down with a load of snow. Looking from our window, the scene was very beautiful and captivating. New Year 2001, would be very special ever for us as our family will be getting completed with the arrival of our son. I had decorated the complete house with decorative skirt lights and prepared ourselves for the big day. The wait was indeed sweet but unbearable.

"Happy Birthday," I wished Anita. The due date was 2 weeks away.

"What fun it would have been if your and baby's birthday would have been on the same day," I told Anita with a random thought.

We looked at each other and said "Shall we go to the hospital now?"

"Dr. Molinari, today is Anita's birthday and we just thought if it is possible to go for the baby today itself?" I called and checked.

"Oh, Happy birthday. Sure, we can try, but not sure if the induced pain will give positive results today itself. If you would have told earlier, we could have planned better," she said.

"No problem, let us try and see. We are reaching hospital" I concluded. We packed our bags and rushed to the hospital.

We reached Worcester Medical Centre, the designated hospital for childbirth, quickly but safely. Anita was admitted to a private room. The room was very spacious with all the facilities for childbirth. It also had a separate section for the attendant's stay.

"We will go for a normal delivery first and then if needed we will try to induce labor. If needed, we will give her an Epidural. We will not go for Caesarean delivery," Dr. Molinari said and asked for our consent.

"Sounds like a good plan. While we hope for today's delivery yet this cannot be at the cost of any risk or operation," we clarified our stand.

"Do you know if it is a boy or girl?" Elina, the nurse, enquired.

"We are going to have a baby boy," I answered with excitement.

"Oh, wonderful. What is the name of the baby boy?" she asked.

"Vatsal Verma," I declared the name of the baby.

We looked at many books and websites to choose the name of our son and found this unique and loving name which meant affectionate, loving. Anita did not get any pain on her birthday. We celebrated her birthday quietly in the hospital room. The next day Anita had severe pain in the back and I was trying to rub her back to help her.

"How much pain women go through, to complete the family." I thought and my respect further increased for women.

And then came the moment and the push started. The practice at Lamaze classes came in handy. I was helping Anita with the breathing exercise. That's why they encourage the partners also to practice it so that during the final moment they can help their partners.

"Sudeep come and help in pulling out the baby," Dr. Molinari asked.

"What, me?" this was unexpected and I got scared with the thought.

"Don't worry, it will be good for you. Do the honors," she insisted.

"Err…Ok," I agreed with a little worry. I did not want to goof up.

I delicately took the head of the baby and started pulling. After some effort and their help, the baby came out drenched in blood.

"Take the scissor and cut the cord," now Elina asked me.

"No, that I won't do. I just can't cut any part of the body," I firmly said.

"Here, look at Vatsal," Elina took the baby and showed it to us.

She cleaned the baby, wrapped him in a warm cloth, and gave it to us.

We were overwhelmed, emotional, speechless, and our hearts filled with love and fulfilment. Little Vatsal has arrived. Our eyes were moist with happiness. Looking at the face of our new-born baby, made us feel nostalgic and full of emotions. Elina then put the baby in an incubator inside our room. Incubators prevent hypothermia by helping the baby maintain an optimal temperature. Temperature controls on a baby incubator can be set manually or automatically based on the baby's temperature. Baby incubators also act as humidifiers. This helps keep the baby from having skin problems.

"Doctor, what can Anita eat as she is feeling hungry?" I asked the Doctor after two hours as Anita was feeling hungry and so was I.

"She can eat anything, she wants," she declared.

"What? No restrictions?" I was a little surprised.

I had seen Doctors in India take precautions and advice light food.

"She can eat a pizza if she wants to," she smiled, looking at us.

"Oh, Wow. Anita, would you like a pizza?" I turned to Anita and asked.

"I would love that," she said with a faint smile.

I went to the main hall in the hospital and bought a big pizza and also bought a few balloons and decorative stuff from the next-door gift shop. Anita ate it with a satisfying expression. I put the balloons all over the room and then had my pizza slices. The room was silent but the emotions in our minds were dancing.

I called my friend Mitesh Raut and took his help to send an email from my account on Vatsal's behalf, announcing his arrival in the world.

"Hello everyone, I am Vatsal, son of Anita and Sudeep Verma. I just wanted to inform you all that, I have just arrived in the world today and I am completely fine and cosy in my incubator. Mom is also doing perfectly fine now and is taking a nap of fulfilment. Dad seems to be gliding in the air with happiness. I need all your blessings and well wishes for our family as we are starting a new journey of love and togetherness. Love and Regards, Vatsal Verma."

This experience left me a changed man. It felt like I have seen so much in so little time and learned a lot from it:

- Females go through a lot during pregnancy and childbirth, this increased my respect. This is why mothers are caring and loving.
- The cycle of birth is fascinating and how wonderful it is to see the transformation of life from a child to adult to mid to old age.
- The reaffirmed belief in and appreciation of a greater power who has designed such a complex process of the life cycle.

"Vatsal has jaundice but can be discharged. He needs to be checked daily. Bring him here daily for next 3 days," Dr. Molinari informed.

"Is this normal? Is there anything to be concerned about?" I asked.

"No, do not worry. It is quite normal. But we have to be careful hence I am asking to bring him to the hospital so that we can ensure his recovery," She sounded confident. I felt a little relaxed but not fully.

In the USA, as per the rules, the kids have to sit in a specific detachable car seat (fixed on top of the car seat). In the infant's car seat child faces backward. It was difficult to bring a two-day infant in a car seat that too facing the back of the car. Vatsal came to our house and made our home complete. We were excited and did our customary rituals. Since Anita was advised to rest, I had to take Vatsal to the hospital, alone in the car, on a very slippery and slanted road. I drove very slowly and carefully with my heart in my mouth. I repeated this exercise thrice before the doctor declared Vatsal fine.

Holy Cross was highly supportive of my being at home and working from home. I received an overwhelming response and congratulatory messages on Vatsal's birth. Family, relatives, friends, colleagues, and all the well-wishers made us feel further overwhelmed. This filled our hearts with love, gratitude, happiness, and positivity. Vatsal had turned three months and we planned celebrations.

And then I received the news of my father's heart attack.

Chapter 31

Three months back it was Anita's father and now it was mine. I felt zapped. Anita asked me to fly to India but it was a *'Dharam Sankat (dilemma)'* for me, as traveling to India leaving a three-month-old kid and wife was a question mark. I was in this dilemma. My local friends Rajesh and Uma called and asked me to move Anita and Vatsal to their home and fly to India. By evening, the news of my father's health spread across to friends in the US and I got calls from all over, asking me to fly to India and they will take care of Anita and Vatsal.

The advice from friends: "Go and see your father at his critical time since Anita and Vatsal can be taken care of here by us. You should not worry since the health of both, Anita and Vatsal are stable now. Instead, you must be at the side of your father. Parents' health improves seeing their kids. We are your family so don't worry."

I felt very humbled with gratitude and could not control my emotions and my eyes got moist. This is my real family away from home. Anita and Vatsal stayed with Srini and Vanaja in Worcester due to the proximity of the Doctor. I took the next available flight to India.

Learning: A true friend is like your true family. At times, a new friend becomes very close, in a short period and this was that moment.

"How are you dad?" I reached India and hugged my father in the bed.

"I am feeling much better seeing you," he answered with a pale smile.

"What is this heart thing, young man?" I tried uplifting his spirit.

"Tell me first, why did you travel this far, leaving Vatsal and Anita?"

"Both of them are doing fine," I gave him confidence.

"But still, you should not have travelled now," he seemed restless.

"I had anyways planned to travel back permanently around this year-end. But had to come to remind you that you have to take care of your health as you have to see your latest grandson," I told him lovingly.

"I will be absolutely fine as I am in good hands here," he told me.

My father had come to my sister, Garima's home, as my brother-in-law, Dr. Sanjay Srivastava, was the divisional medical officer (DMO), northern railways, and he could get the best medical attention here. Dr. Sanjay had a very strong connection and network with all the reputed doctors in Kanpur. A thorough heart diagnosis of my father was performed and the best heart surgeon was seeing him, personally. As per diagnosis, there were blockages in the arteries. Looking at the age and other health factors, the surgery was not recommended, instead, the decision was to keep him on medication. His health started improving.

He has very rich experience in his life and is very proud about that. I engaged him in his real-life experiences so that he feels good about it.

"I also am going to publish a book of your poetry, describing various places of Dev Bhoomi in Uttar Pradesh hills," I told him.

My father was an officer in Uttar Pradesh Tourism (when Uttarakhand was part of UP), he travelled various places in the hills and described the importance of all these places through his poetry. I knew that these poetries are very close to his heart and seeing a book published out of it will make him very happy. I knew that when he is happy, he becomes a fighter which was the need of the hour for his health.

"That will be good. You can share the book with your friends so that they can understand the importance of these places," he sparked.

"Yes dad, sure. This is a rich experience and must be shared," I agreed.

The thought crossed in my mind that I also have many interesting learnings 'On the Curves of my Life' and someday, I shall share it too.

The next few days flew by and I was happy and satisfied to see his improvement. Nothing is more important than being with parents at the time of need. I felt that I need to come back to India sooner.

I flew back to the USA, after spending 10 days with my father in India. I expressed my heartfelt gratitude to Srini and Vanaja for being family away from home. These are the moments, when one discovers true friends who act more than a family at the time of need. With my worry gone, I was delighted to see Vatsal grow.

I discussed with Anita the plan of action to move back to India sooner. We decided that the September timeframe will be good. I informed leaders at Holy Cross about my plan and assessed the status of the projects at hand. I created execution as well as a handover plan for a smooth transition. After two months of crazy work we were in control.

With three months left to move to India, we decided to take Vatsal, on his first road trip, from Boston to Toronto, since, I wanted to take Vatsal to my mentor, PK's place who lived in Toronto. Worcester to Toronto is about 825 km. We drove to Buffalo (671 Km) first without Vatsal giving any problem and stayed there. We took a Canadian visa from the Canadian consulate in Buffalo and crossed the border into Canada the following day. We then drove to Toronto smoothly and reached PK's house. I was super happy realizing that Vatsal also has the same love of traveling as that of his father, grandfather, and great grandfather. "Life is going to be fun with this little fellow!" I thought. We met Sonia didi (PK's wife) and kids, Rishika and Rishi along with PK. We stayed in Toronto for three days and then came back.

We organized get-togethers in the next few months with friends from Foundation, Raymond, and local neighbors. Many friends flew or drove from various places to our home– Sameer Munje & Preeti, Ramesh Gopal & Lavanya, Venugopal Iyer & Suchitra, Mitesh Raut, and Seema Power. Another get-together was with Raymond friends like – Ravi Ghantasala, Kannan Nambiar & Anu , and a few others.

Bill (William Conley), Director of HR in College of the Holy Cross, was my true friend, supporter, customer, and leader. He organized a farewell party for me at his house around two weeks before our departure. It was an overwhelming experience as many colleagues from Holy Cross had gathered and we were given very special treatment and many gifts. My true American friends in the United States had been wonderful to me and I was going to miss them but will cherish our friendship forever.

With two days to go, I sold my car and cancelled my credit card, and closed the bank accounts. We started packing and it was difficult to decide, what to take with us and what to leave behind. With great difficulty, we discarded many items but still ended up with 13 bags including the cabin luggage. Rest of the stuff we either gave to friends or donated to the red cross. We had booked a British Airways flight from Boston to Delhi via London on 12th September 2001.

My final farewell was planned for 11th September, a day before my departure at Holy Cross. The big farewell started at 8:00 AM in the conference room with a lot of food and drinks. Everyone had gathered and the atmosphere was very good with people sharing their experience with me and I was getting a lot of compliments.

"Please turn on the TV right now"
Maureen entered and said in a huff.

Chapter 32

9:00 AM, 11th September 2001 (HR Conference Room at Holy Cross)

"**One Tower of the World Trade Centre has been hit by an airplane**". The news channel was broadcasting the news. We saw the tower was burning with heavy smoke and fire erupting out of it.

SHOCKING!!!

"Oh My God. Shit. What the f… No. This can't be true," there was an immediate reaction of shock and despair in the conference room. We all were shell-shocked and could not believe what we were seeing.

"The plane has hit North Tower at around 8:46 AM. It is not yet confirmed what kind of plane it was and from where this came," the news anchor was reporting in shock.

None of us was speaking as we could not digest what we were seeing.

9:03 AM Boom. Another plane appeared and hit the 2nd WTC tower. While watching the huge smoke erupting from the North Tower, we saw another plane suddenly appear and hit the South Tower of the World Trade Centre. A huge ball of fire appeared from the floors where the plane has hit.

"Oh my God, that looks like a second plane. I just saw another plane exploded in the south tower?" the news anchor exclaimed in shock.

"Oh My God. Oh, God. It looks on purpose," they blubbered.

We all were shell shocked but this time with huge worry. We were watching this Live on TV. There was a huge commotion in the room. People started expressing shock, dismay and many were in tears.

"Oh My God. What the hell. Nooooo. Gowwd. What the fuck?"

The direction of the plane was such that it came hitting directly into the WTC South Tower. Someone said that it seems that the plane has hit on purpose. And that is how we also felt in the conference room. Suddenly, we all were concerned for the well-being of our known ones in the Manhattan area. People started calling the ones they knew in that area. I also realized that I had two of my friends working in that area but I was not sure if they worked exactly in WTC or nearby buildings. I called both of them but their phones were not reachable. Finally, I came to know that one of the two friends, I was looking for, was working in the One Liberty Plaza building which was right across WTC. In the conference room, only a few people were able to connect to the ones they were looking for. We all realized that either network has gone down or has been deliberately blocked. In between, unconfirmed news started coming that the flights had been hijacked but nothing was confirmed at that time. A lot of speculation was going on but most people had started speculating that this may be a terrorist attack. I called Anita and after sharing the terrible news, I asked her to watch the TV so that she is aware of what is happening.

9:30 AM: President Bush addresses Americans, saying that "Today, we've had a national tragedy," he started. "Two airplanes have crashed into the World Trade Centre in an apparent terrorist attack on our country" and leads to a moment of silence.

This confirmed that the plane crash was indeed a terrorist attack. News channels started flashing the news of 'America

Under Attack'. Feeling in the conference room was that of shock and dismay.

9:40 AM: "Pentagon is hit by the third plane. America under attack"

And suddenly, the panic started spreading among the people in the room. All the hits were unbelievable. None of us could believe that WTC towers can be hit but now Pentagon has been hit. These events were too much to digest and I was in complete shock and horror.

The news kept on unfolding. The next news was that all the flights had been grounded. I felt this was a good action as more and more flights in the air would mean more worries and more possible attacks. The live television coverage of the smoke and fire spreading in the upper floors of the twin WTC towers was horrible and it looked very difficult to stop the fire. There were reports that people had been trying to come out from both the towers. Some people, on phone from WTC, inform their loved ones that they are stuck inside. It was very disturbing and unnerving. We hoped that people can be rescued.

9:59 AM: "The South Tower, of the twin TWC, started collapsing"

The way the tower was falling, felt like something made of light material falling easily. The truth was that the building was made of solid steel and iron and burning something of that sort was unimaginable in the wildest of the dreams. It was like a castle of cards getting destroyed. Huge smoke started spreading while the building was coming down many floors together at a time. And within a matter of few seconds, the majority of the tower was down, turning into rubble. It was understandable that many people must have died as earlier there was news of a lot of people stuck inside.

AN UNIMAGINABLE AND HORRIBLE VIEW TO WATCH LIVE ON TV.

10:05 AM: "Another airplane has crashed near Pennsylvania"

No further details were available about this crash at that time. While we were watching the events, live on TV, in dismay and shock, the news came that another airplane has crashed near Pennsylvania. As we were getting news of continuous shocks, one after the other, we did not know what else is in store in time to come for all of us.

10:15 AM: "Pentagon's outer ring wall collapsing"

The news of the symbol of American strength and control getting down was demoralizing. News started coming in that this is a terrorist attack so we were dismayed by the large scale of the attack.

10:28 AM: "North Tower of the twin TWC towers started collapsing" just like the first one after burning for almost 102 minutes. It was like a repeat of the first tower collapse.

More unconfirmed news and speculation that many more persons may have been buried and died. This was the most horrible thing that I had ever seen in my life with so much horror and destruction. The smoke and dust spread in a very wide area and the nearby buildings were also evacuated due to the security and safety of people nearby.

Falling debris from the towers, combined with fire, in several surrounding buildings, led to the collapse of all the buildings in the complex and caused catastrophic damage to other large structures.

World Trade Centre

The World Trade Centre was a large complex of seven buildings in the Financial District of Lower Manhattan, New

York City, United States. It opened on April 4, 1973. At the time of completion, the Twin Towers—the 1st World Trade Centre (the North Tower), at 1,368 feet (417 m), and 2nd World Trade Centre (the South Tower), at 1,362 feet (415.1 m)—were the tallest buildings in the world. Other buildings in the complex included the Marriott World Trade Centre (3 WTC), 4 WTC, 5 WTC, 6 WTC, and 7 WTC. The complex was built between 1966-1975, by Minoru Yamasaki as lead architect and Emery Roth & Sons as associate architects, for $400 million (equivalent to $2.27 billion in 2021). Earlier also, the World Trade Centre experienced several major incidents, including a fire in February 1975, a bombing in February 1993, and a bank robbery in January 1998. But this was an act of terror. I was still not able to digest it. In a matter of just 1.5 hours, the complete WTC got demolished.

I had visited WTC thrice in the last 5 years, the first time when I went to join Foundation Software in April 1997, after lending from India, the second time in 1998, and the last time in 1999. Such a beautiful landmark. All memories of my earlier visit flashed back in my mind. I remembered visiting the top floor from where one can see the breath-taking view of the complete Manhattan area, Statue of Liberty, and far-off places. The feeling of being at the top of the world's tallest building was out of the world. Seeing the towers falling felt horrible.

"All the flights had been grounded and the airports closed", the news came. Details started coming about the flights that had been used.

- American Airlines Flight 11 (Boeing 767) with 81 passengers and 11 crew members, departed from Logan International Airport in **Boston** and crashed into the North Tower (1 WTC) at 8:46 AM

- United Airlines Flight 175 (Boeing 767) with 56 passengers and 9 crew members, departed from Logan International Airport in **Boston** and crashed into the North Tower (2 WTC) at 9:03 AM
- American Airlines Flight 77 (Boeing 757) with 58 passengers and 6 crew members, departs from Washington Dulles International Airport and crashed into The Pentagon at 9:37 AM
- United Airlines Flight 93 (Boeing 757) with 37 passengers and 7 crew members, departs 42 minutes late from Newark International Airport and crashed near Pennsylvania

I just noticed that two out of the four flights had flown from Boston. Immediately, I remembered that our flight to India tomorrow is also from the Boston airport. But the airport has been shut down.

"Oh My God, what about our flight?"
I panicked with this realization.

Chapter 33

Days of Horror, Uncertainty, Frustration and Wait

September 11th, 2001

Anita was watching, the company-provided television in the living room, on the ground floor, when I came home. We had sold the television that we had in our bedroom on the first floor.

"This is horrible, I am not able to understand how can this happen?" Anita asked as soon as I came back from the office.

"This is unbelievable, shocking, horrible and an inhuman act. The whole situation seems like a horrible dream," I was very concerned.

"My heart is crying to see people dying in this horrifying scenario. And God knows how many of them have died or got hurt in WTC and nearby towers. And those poor passengers and crew members inside the crashed planes," I was shaking with what I had witnessed.

"Situation is very volatile and we don't know what will happen," I told.

"Both the planes that have crashed in twin WTC towers and have caused so much damage had flown from Boston's Logan International airport. Same place from where our flight is scheduled to fly tomorrow afternoon. And now Boston airport has been shut down and all the flights have been grounded," I drew Anita's attention to our issue.

"Oh My God, yes. What will happen now?" she sounded very scared.

"God knows. As per the current situation, I don't think airports will open in which case we may not be able to fly tomorrow," I spoke.

"Oh shit. So, what will we do then?" she asked

"I have no clue. We will have to watch the situation and just pray to God that this nonsense stops and normalcy returns soon. But it seems very difficult that the situation will be normal soon," I responded.

We put a bedsheet on the carpet in the drawing-room, in front of the television, and got glued to television with our phone lying next to us.

Reports started coming in:

- Speculations that UA Flight 93 that crashed in Pennsylvania was probably heading towards Capitol building or The White house.
- 10:49 AM: CNN reports that a mass evacuation of Washington, D.C., and New York has been started.
- 10:50 AM Five stories part of the Pentagon collapse due to fire.
- 11:00 AM International flights headed to the US diverted to Canada.
- 11:16: American Airlines confirms the loss of its two aircraft.
- 11:53 United Airlines confirms the loss of its two aircraft.
- 11:55 AM U.S. border with Mexico is put on highest alert.

The focus of the news on various channels was going towards the collapse of the twin towers of WTC. Huge rescue work was in progress.

- 12:01 PM: Fourteen people, including twelve firefighters, who were in the North Tower, climbed the stairs and came out alive.
- 12:04 PM: Los Angeles International Airport, the intended destination of Flights 11, 77, and 175, is shut down.
- 12:15 PM: San Francisco International Airport, the intended destination of Flight 93, is shut down.
- 12:16 PM: The airspace over the United States is clear of all commercial and private flights.
- 12:39 PM: A senator characterizes the attack as an "act of war."
- 12:41 PM: A senator tells CNN, "Both the FBI and our intelligence community believe that this is Bin Laden's signature."
- 01:04 PM: President Bush puts the U.S. military on high alert worldwide. President stated that "freedom itself was attacked this morning by a faceless coward and freedom will be defended. The United States will hunt down and punish those, responsible."
- 01:27 PM: Washington DC Mayor, declares a state of emergency.
- 04:00 PM: High officials in the federal intelligence community are stating that Osama bin Laden is suspect number one.
- 05:20 PM: 7 World Trade Centre, a 47-story building, collapses.
- 06:00 PM: Explosions and tracer fires are reported in Kabul

- 06:00 PM: The last of the aircraft headed for the U.S. lands in Canada at Vancouver Airport, since it was flying over the Pacific.
- 07:30 PM: the U.S. denies responsibility for explosions in Kabul.

In the meanwhile, efforts to locate survivors in the rubble that had been the twin towers continued. The WTC collapse became known as "Ground Zero." Relatives and friends of victims or likely victims, started gathering, many displaying photographs of the missing.

08:30 PM: Excerpts of President Bush's addresses to the country:

- "Today, our fellow citizens, our way of life, our very freedom came under attack in a series of deliberate and deadly terrorist acts."
- "Terrorist attacks can shake the foundations of our biggest buildings, but they cannot touch America's foundation. These acts shatter steel, but they can't dent the steel of American resolve."
- "The search is underway for those who are behind these evil acts. We will make no distinction between the terrorists who committed these acts and those who harbor them."

Though, I was almost sure that the possibility of our flight from Boston to London may not take off, yet I called the British Airways.

"As of now, all the flights have been cancelled till further notice. Boston airport is not operating and none of our flights can take off till we get clearance. I am afraid, we do not have any further information at this time," the British Airways customer service agent responded.

Anita and I looked at each other with a feeling of uncertainty, disappointment, helplessness, and horror.

We were so much looking forward to going back to India and had prepared ourselves completely.

"We have sold out the car, withdrew our credit card, closed our bank accounts. Even we do not have any groceries left at home," I spoke.

"We have food till tomorrow but will have to arrange from outside if we have to stay any longer, as the situation seems to be," she replied.

"Let us wait till tomorrow and see how things unfold. We will do something about it," I tried to assure her.

We stayed glued to the TV. The TV was on, the whole night, and we took our nap in between as neither we were getting sound sleep nor did we want to miss any news. We were relieved that no other unfortunate news came that night and hoped for better days ahead.

September 12th, 2001

News channels were still focusing on showing rescue work at the WTC as well as the next possible response from the United States. For the first time in U.S. history, the emergency preparedness plan was invoked, closing the airspace for all international flights thus stranding tens of thousands of passengers across the world. This meant, about five hundred flights to be turned back or redirected to other countries. Canada received 226 of the diverted flights and launched Operation Yellow Ribbon to deal with large numbers of grounded and stranded passengers. The whole world was impacted by this horrible incident. The attacks had a significant economic impact on the USA and world markets. The stock exchanges did not open on 11th and 12th.

Within hours of the attacks, the FBI released the names and, in many cases, the personal details of the suspected pilots and hijackers. Most of them were from the middle east countries and mostly from Saudi Arabia and were suspected of having connections with Al Qaeda. This information had sparked many debates and while people were very angry yet this injected fear amongst many immigrant Asian communities.

"How are you doing Sudeep and how are Anita and Vatsal?" William Conley (Bill) called me to check our well-being.

"We are very much in shock and still can't believe what has happened," I responded in a low voice.

"We all are. This is a cowardly act and will be responded to," he spoke.

"Your flights must have been rescheduled, right?" he asked.

"Yes, that was expected yesterday itself. I had called the airlines and they also do not know when they will start operating. They are waiting for clarity from the government," I shared the status.

"That may take a few days at least. So how are you holding up at home? Do you need anything? Can I help you?" he was concerned.

"We had finished all the food items. We may need some items from grocery stores for a few more days till we get next flight," I spoke.

"No problem. I know you do not have a car, so, I will come and take you to the grocery store," he graciously offered.

"That will be highly appreciated. You are my savior," I thanked him.

Bill took me to the grocery store. I purchased food for a week.

September 13th, 2001

Numerous incidents of harassment and hate crimes against Muslims and South Asians were reported following the attacks. The terrorists included commercial pilots from Saudi Arabia and others, who had pursued flight training in the United States, officials said. Across the United States, FBI and U.S. Treasury Department agents fanned out looking for any connections between passenger lists, intercepted cell phone calls, and suspects. There were many arrests, along with a raid on a Boston hotel room used by the terrorists. Police earlier found a rental car at Logan Airport that contained Arabic-language airplane flight instructions. The investigations were going in full flow.

September 14th, 2001

The news of some airports opening and some domestic flights resuming gave us much-needed hope and we kept our fingers crossed and prayed for its early opening. Boston, being the centre of all the terrorist action, was still closed. Bush administration was getting ready for a full-scale assault on terror. U.S. allies were getting aligned together to launch a great retaliation. With time, the grief was getting converted into anger among the residents. This resulted in growing hate crimes across the country. The anger was in general against the Asians especially the middle east. But since there is a lot of similarity among the natives of this region hence people were not able to make a distinction and as a result, many people from other countries of the region were also getting targeted.

"We are living in a secluded home among the native Americans, with no Indians or Asians anywhere near," Anita raised the concern.

"That is true. Though people here are very nice and amazing, yet the times are such that everyone is very angry. And sometimes anger leads to an unintentional act too," I was also worried.

"Our house has only glass windows which can be broken very easily if someone wants to," she raised further concern.

"Let's close all the curtains, switch off the lights and watch the TV at a low volume. And let us be vigil. That's all we can do," I responded.

We were scared and felt the importance of our homeland. Feelings of Rebel & Retaliation were looking tiny and small in front of this.

We felt: "*Jaan hai to Jahan hai*
(If you have life, you have world.)"

Chapter 34

September 15th, 2001

Hate Crimes grew across the country. We heard that the Sikhs were also targeted because Sikh males usually wear turbans, which were sometimes confused with Muslims. There were reports of attacks on mosques and other religious buildings (even a Hindu temple), and assaults on people, including the murder of a Sikh mistaken for a Muslim, who was fatally shot on September 15, 2001, in Mesa, Arizona. This news made us further nervous and worried, especially since we did not see any news of international flights starting from Boston or any nearby major airports including New York, Newark, or Chicago. With growing anger and hate crimes, the situation was becoming very bad in the country specifically for Asians in general. Though, we were living in a secluded place, and in an accommodation provided by the College of the Holy Cross which was considered safe, yet we are Asians and there was always a possibility of getting mistaken as someone else.

A friend called and told me that there is news that flights from Toronto may go to India via Europe. This was like a ray of light in a long dark tunnel to us. We started deliberating if we leave all our stuff here and take some kind of ground transportation to reach the Canada border and reach Toronto and try to catch that flight. But we got worried that traveling on road would mean getting exposed for hours and hence the possibility of a hate crime. We dropped the plan.

We felt helpless, frustrated, unsettled, and angry due to this.

President Bush addresses the nation on Radio: Key points were:

"I am engaged in extensive sessions with members of my National Security Council, as we plan a comprehensive assault on terrorism."

"This will be a different kind of conflict against a different kind of enemy. Those who make war against the United States have chosen their destruction. Victory against terrorism will not take place in a single battle, but in a series of decisive actions..."

"A terrorist attack designed to tear us apart has instead bound us together as a nation. Over the past few days, we have learned much about American courage -- the courage of firefighters and police officers who suffered so great a loss, the courage of passengers aboard United 93 who may well have fought with the hijackers...."

"I will not settle for a token act. Our response must be sweeping, sustained, and effective. We have much to do, and much to ask of the American people."

I thought, "plans were being made for a sustained campaign against perpetrators and terrorism. War in the middle east may close the air space over it. **This may reduce the possibility of flight back to home**".

September 16th, 2001

We were not able to sleep properly so that we do not miss any important information and instead took intermittent naps only. Groceries were running out faster and the fresh milk for Vatsal as well.

Bright Ray of Hope

I got the news that British Airways is planning to start its flight from Logan International airport on 18th September 2001. This was a HUGE ray of hope for us and I immediately started calling British Airways customer service numbers as well as Booking office numbers. But all the numbers were busy continuously.

These were desperate times and hence I just kept calling the numbers with some patience. Though, I was very worried that the longer it will take to connect to them, the lesser possibility it will be for me to get any seats available on the flight on 18th September. We just wanted to get out of this situation on 18th September itself.

After trying for around 40 minutes, I finally got connected to the booking office of British Airways.

"I had my booking on 12th September on British Airways from Boston to London and then a connecting flight from London to Delhi. I would like to take the very first flight out of Boston," I explained the details.

"Unfortunately, all flights on the 18th are already booked. The next available flight is on 21st September 2001, I can book that," she told.

"But I need to reach India urgently and am already late," I pleaded.

"Wait sir, let me see what I can do for you," she put me on hold.

"Sorry sir, but there is no flight to Delhi. I can get you to London on the 18th flight, but from there, I can only send you to Mumbai, as all Delhi flights are booked," she gave me the option after a while.

"That's fine. Please book us on Boston-London-Mumbai," I grabbed it.

Finally, a flight to India was booked. We took a huge sigh of relief.

September 17th, 2001

There were constant reports of hate crimes from various parts of the country. I heard from a few people that residents are not able to differentiate Indians from the Middle East country people and as a result, they are given bad looks and also sometimes abusive comments. The situation was not good and there was a constant risk. Now that the flights were booked, we felt some relief but wanted to ensure that we remain inside the house and do not venture out.

On the other hand, as per speculations, a possible retaliation from the United States against the perpetrators could take place anytime.

We were worried that in case of a war in the middle east or Afghanistan, the air space may get closed, jeopardizing our flights. We kept praying for our well-being and our safe return. I thought in the worst case, we will fly from the west side of the USA via Japan.

I received news that there are new security measures implemented at the airports and that everything including pieces of baggage is getting checked thoroughly. I got this confirmation from the airlines.

Earlier, we had packed 13 bags after great optimization. But looking at the current situation we wanted to take the allowed limit of 9 bags (6 check-ins and 3 handbags) only. We started luggage optimization again and decided to leave a lot of clothes and decorative items, etc. We finally had optimized to ten bags including one laptop bag as allowed. At this time, nothing was more important for us than to reach back to India safely, everything else was mere material as we realized. We were very happy about our optimization and were all set for the flight. We decided to give away two big bags of clothes to the Red Cross or the Salvation Army. We asked our friends to take the bags as well as decorative items.

"Hi Anita, how are you and how is Vatsal?" Pat Morrisette called.

"We are doing perfectly fine Pat, thanks for calling," Anita replied.

"That sounds good. Did you hear anything from airlines?" Pat asked.

"Yes, we just got confirmation of the flight tomorrow afternoon. There were no flights available for Delhi on 18th, yet they got us seats to Mumbai which is ok for us and we have booked it," Anita said.

"Oh, that's wonderful. You must be feeling fine now," Pat was happy.

"Yes Pat, very much indeed," Anita responded with a big sigh of relief.

"Can I do anything for you guys? Do you need fresh milk for Vatsal?" Pat asked with concern.

"We are all set. Fresh milk for Vatsal is over but we will try to manage," Anita said not wanting to bother Pat.

"No worries, I will come and get fresh milk from the market," Pat said.

"Aww, how can we thank you ever," Anita said with gratitude.

Pat brought fresh milk for Vatsal. We talked for a while before she left.

We felt so grateful and did not have words to express our gratitude.

Learnings: Our American friends were more than a family to us. They were the true friends in need. What if the whole of humanity believes in love and acts accordingly? We indeed were fortunate to have received love from so many friends who became my family.

September 18th, 2001

The whole night we could not sleep and kept watching TV, praying, nothing untoward happens and we return safely to home, tomorrow.

Friends came in the morning, and I gave them big bags of clothes and other items and requested to donate them to the Salvation Army or Red Cross wherever they find it convenient. I also gave one bag, with decorative and other items, to them which I had purchased with great interest but under current circumstances did not want to take back.

I called William Conly and Pat Morrissette and shared my gratitude very emotionally. I always had felt like they were my real family, in America, home away from home. It was a very heartfelt emotional moment for me and I was running short of words for gratitude.

We had heard that there is very strict security and were advised to reach the airport early hence we planned to reach there around 5 hours ahead of time. As we were entering the airport premises, we saw very long lines which made us very curious and nervous. We came to know that all these lines are actually for the departure passengers. With so much luggage with us, along with little Vatsal, it was very difficult to manage but the urge of going back was so much that it did not matter to us as long as we take our flight. Marshals and their K9 dogs were everywhere and checking everything.

After a wait of around two hours finally, we reached the check-in counters. We were told that no handbags are allowed. We were zapped. They asked to book all the luggage except a baby bag. All our valuables and laptops were booked in a hurry. One Marshal asked Anita to even taste the milk in Vatsal's bottle which she did.

Finally, we boarded the flight;
After a delay of an hour, it took off.

Chapter 35

The year 2001

"Jaan bachi, laakhon paye (Life saved is worth gaining millions)," the moment we were out of American air space, Anita and I looked at each other with a sense of relief. And then, we looked at each other saying: "Laut ke buddhu ghar ko *chale* (Fools returning to home.)"

This was the first time we could afford a smile after eight dreadful days. We were on the first seats of the economy class, and the air hostesses had given a bassinet for Vatsal which was attached to the wall opposite us. We had made sure that he does not sleep for hours so that he can sleep without problem during the flight.

The only slight worry left in our mind was that the airspace over the middle east, Afghanistan, Pakistan should not get closed due to a possible war, so that we can reach India safely and peacefully. We had not slept for days except for a couple of hours of nap. I wanted to take a nap, but instead, I reflected on the experiences while sailing through the curves of my life in the 13 years.

Not qualifying in the competitive exams was the prime reason for my criticism. Being emotional, I took this change of behavior of society to my heart, becoming a rebel starting a retaliation.

But now, when I look back at my journey after starting my retaliation, I realized that besides criticism and rejection, I also got a lot of support from many people from the society throughout the curves of my life at various stages:

- I met my Mentor, PK, who gave me timely valuable Advice and helped me immensely throughout

- My best friend, Vivek Verma, gave me realistic Advice which helped me choose the right track in life instead of giving up
- My family- mother, father, wife, son, sisters, brother, brothers-in-law, sister-in-law, nieces, and nephews always supported me.
- My backbone, my close friends always supported me.
- I met so many new people in all the organizations I worked for, who helped and supported me immensely.
- My dearest friends in Holy Cross William Conley, Pat Morrissette who helped in our real moments of crisis as well.
- I made many friends during my stay in the US who became like a family to me and supported me immensely.

I realized, that I had been really lucky to have such amazing support from so many well-wishers during my Retaliation as a Rebel and even before that. These well-wishers gave me a very valuable advice which changed my life for the good and I learned so many invaluable lessons.

"I will always be grateful to these angels in my life," I felt humble.

Our British Airways flight landed in London and we had crossed the first major hurdle to safety. It was so heartening to see Vatsal did not make any fuss on the flight. We boarded the connecting flight to Mumbai after a wait of a couple of hours and the flight took off. I tried to go back to the reflections, to understand the outcome.

I started questioning myself and tried to find answers:

'Why did I become a Rebel and pursue my Retaliation?' *I analysed.*

Dreams getting shattered due to someone's mischievous act.

Wrongly accused of cheating; Attack on values.

Change in the attitude of society; Criticism by even close people.

Wrong perception of betrayal by Kalpana's mother.

Getting dumped without being understood.

Realization that society respects materialistically successful people by and large.

All the above incidents, one after another shattered me and I became very angry. Anger clouds a clear thought process and makes a person think from a negative perspective. Hence, instead of making a positive journey of excelling, I took the approach of a rebel and started my journey of retaliation.

"Why did I not focus on my well-wishers and instead focused on those who rejected me?" I further tried to comprehend.

"I could not understand, how material success can be a factor of change in the opinion of liking or disliking someone. I was shocked and angry. In this state of anger and agony, I just wanted to prove them wrong. With this myopic state of mind, I could not realize that I was still loved by many well-wishers. Anger takes away the ability to see the positive side. Negativity can never be the right approach."

Realization: "It takes all types of people to make this world. There will always be people who will criticize. Trying situations make us myopic and negative and we lose our focus from well-wishers and positivity."

"Was it worth pursuing the path of being a Rebel with Retaliation?"

While, I strongly believe that being a good human being is more important yet that is not enough. In practicality, it's important to be materialistically successful as well, specifically, since most of us do not have the strong willpower to ignore criticism. It is absolutely fine to pursue one's passion, irrespective of materialism if one does not care about the criticism of society. Since, I am a people person, who cannot be ignorant, pursuing the journey of growth was the right move. However, it should not have been as a rebel with retaliation.

Take Away: "Kuch to log kahenge, logo ka kaam hai kehna…"

"Am I a changed person now?" I smiled and looked at myself.

"I am a changed person with more insight and fantastic experiential learning. I believe in **Purposeful Perseverance with Patience, Passion, Positivity and Play realize the Power of self, achieve Pride, and ultimately Progress in life**. The **success and recognition** at work gave me much-needed **confidence**. The **love and support** of people made me full of **gratitude. Advice from well-wishers** changed my outlook."

"*Bharat Mata ki Jai*", we all cheered as the plane landed in Mumbai.

I took a deep breath of relief. I have survived successfully.

Various Shades of experiential learning positively enriched my life and my perseverance helped me sail through the curves of my life.

"Life Never gives up on those who Never give up on Life."

And the journey continues…

Takeaways of the Book

"Life is the biggest **teacher** and the **experiences** are the real **lessons.**"

Thirteen Years of Experience and Thirteen Shades of Lessons On the Curves of My Life

1. Find The Mentor: 'Seek Jamvant' and 'Find Hanuman' within.
2. Seek The Advice: Take the 'Right' Advice on the curves of life.
3. The Success: Often gap from failure to success is minuscule.
4. The Opportunity: Identify & Ride the Wave of Right Opportunity.
5. The Dream: Dreams can change; New Opportunity = New Dream.
6. The Self Confidence: A big differentiator on the path of success.
7. The Courage: It is never too late to do anything.
8. The Formula = Take Initiative, Identify Problem, Create Solution. (Initiative+Curiosity)+(Creativity+Innovation) = Learning+Growth.
9. The Excellence with fun: Ensures sustainable, Enjoyable journey.
10. The Magnificent P's: My Experiential Life Mantra for success.
11. The Power of Self: Yog Nidra discovered on the curves of my life.
12. The Obstruction: Kuchh toh log kahenge, Logo ka kaam hai kehna.
13. The Perspective: Theory of Relativity; Change is the only Constant

Find The Mentor: 'Seek Jamvant' and 'Find Hanuman' within.

We all have a lot of potential in us but often we do not get the right guidance at the right time. This results in not realizing our potential. I learned the importance of a Guru, Mentor, Coach quite late in life.

My life changed with the entry of my mentor, PK. He steered my career in the right direction with his valuable advice, suggestions, and guidance. His advice to go for specialization in advanced technologies proved to be a fantastic beginning. When I wanted to move to the USA for my quick growth, he gave me fantastic guidance as well as opportunities. I could never have succeeded in the IFAS project without his guidance, encouragement, and faith in me. When, I got the Foundation Software offer, I did not know about PeopleSoft and since I already had another offer, I thought of rejecting this offer. PK's guidance made me understand the importance of ERP which changed my growth trajectory drastically upwards. His guidance and encouragement helped me identify my true potential and enhanced my growth significantly. That is the difference a mentor brings in one's life. Mentors can be many. One shall always keep on looking for them.

Learnings– Find a mentor in life to find your potential and direction Find your Mentor who can guide, motivate, support, and tell you about the possibilities, opportunities, and uncover the **power in You**. It was Jamvant who helped Hanuman identify his powers. Like Jamvant, a mentor helps identify potential & guides to the right path.

Seek The Advice: Take 'Right' Advice on the curves of life

I sought and received many advice in life that immensely helped me:

- Vivek Verma: **Materialistic achievement is practically important**.
- MC Gaur: The power of self. This Instilled much needed **self-belief**.
- PK: Advanced technology **specialization** is vital for quick growth.
- PK: **Tough situations result in best learnings** (IFAS Project).
- Aryender Sharma: **Fight till the end** instead of giving up.
- PK: **Yog Nidra for quick rejuvenation while working hard**.
- PK: **Every opportunity must be deliberated** before the decision.

These were just a few advice, which benefited me immensely.

Learning: Seek and Deliberate Advice

Seek advice from a mentor, guru, expert, well-wisher. There can be many advice and should be deliberated upon. Finally, it is your responsibility to take the final decision. Often, we are either biased or get ignorant about certain things. These advices give us new learning, new perspective, opens new horizons and change the path of our journey in a much better direction, like it did for me with above mentioned experiences in my life. However, people give advice from their own knowledge and experiences and at times it may not be relevant for others. Hence evaluate and understand the advice and then take appropriate action of following or not following. But every advice is an opportunity to think with respect to self.

The Success: Often the gap from failure to success is minuscule

One of the biggest lessons I learned at Raymond (RCS) was to not give up. This instilled immense confidence and perseverance in me:

- I was given the Financial Accounting project as a project manager. The previous project team had resigned and I was asked to take over. I did not had the domain knowledge but accepted the challenge. We did not have the right handover and struggled. We had very tough timelines and were stressed working 24X7. Just five days before Go Live programs produced wrong results. In frustration and stress, we thought of giving up and leave RCS.
- **The advice** from the leader was ***"You have worked so hard till now, you still have few days, do not give up until you fight till the end. This way at least you still can succeed. If you give up now, you will always regret the failure and the thought– what if I would have tried more and succeeded."***
- **Working with a calm mind**, we achieved success the very next day.

Within a day, perspective changed from giving up to a huge success.

Learning: Perseverance, Patience; Never Give up till the end

Giving up without trying till end is a failure anyways. Persevering till the last moment with patience and positivity may give success. Often due to lack of visibility we are not able to see the gap between giving up and succeeding. Try till the last mile with patience is the mantra.

The Opportunity: Identify and Ride the Wave of 'Right' Opportunities

Most of the time we have a plethora of opportunities around us but we are not able to identify them either due to lack of knowledge, guidance, or sheer ignorance. Often this means missing an opportunity that could have changed our life for good. Opportunities can be identified accidentally or through research or through the guidance of an expert. Predictable opportunities can come through an expert or self-search. Some of the opportunities on my curves were:

- Accidental Opportunity: A failure in the engineering exam accidentally showed me my dream career in ISRO through physics.
- Self-researched Opportunity: Detailed search showed an opportunity to grow fast in high in demand Information Technology
- Expert-guided Opportunity: PK's advice to ride the wave of specialized in-demand technologies.
- Accidental Opportunity: PeopleSoft offer from Foundation Software. I bumped into it by chance. It changed my life immensely for good.
- Initiative Opportunity: Be curious; Take initiative; Identify the problem; Create a solution; Make an impact. Like Raymond ERP.

Learnings: Identify the opportunities; Ride the early wave

Develop an eye to identifying an opportunity. Talk to mentors, seniors, and experts to keep a tab on the latest trend and then grab the opportunity which is relevant for your growth. There indeed is no dearth of opportunities if we develop an eye to identify them.

The Dream: Dream can change; New Opportunity maybe New Dream

A dream is a cherished aspiration, ambition, or ideal. For some people these dreams remain constant but often with the progress of life, exposure, knowledge and experience, the aspirations and ambitions change and so does dreams. Sometimes, like in my case, one does not realize actual aspiration or ambition but accidently finds it. Like, I found my dream career in Physics. For some people, who still want to pursue the same aspiration or dream but somehow the aspiration is not met or the dream is shattered then that does not mean that it is the end of the road. Because aspirations do change and newer dreams get created with newer opportunities in life. In my case, after physics, I found new aspiration in the information technology space and pursued that aspiration and ambition.

Learning: There are many opportunities – Observe, Identify & Grab

Dreams can change based on the changed scenario, aspiration, knowledge and experience. One shall never get demoralised if due to some reason one cannot achieve a dream. Rather the new opportunities are a source of creating new dreams and one shall be very observant about this fact. Getting stuck with a dream, even if it does not make sense with changed time, may not be fruitful. New formula in my opinion is that every new opportunity may be a source of a new aspiration and dream.

The Self Confidence: A big differentiator on the path of success

Self-confidence is one of the biggest differentiators of a successful and happy person. People with poor self-confidence are pessimistic, shy, indecisive, feel unlovable, sarcastic, poor risk-taker, non-assertive and lack taking initiative. There are many causes of poor self-confidence like poor self-image, being neglected, criticism, betrayal, failure, discouragement, trauma, and fear of "what will people say". Lack of self-confidence results in poor performance, distorting views of self/others and leads to being unhappy, professionally and personally.

Few failures in education, broken love life and criticism by society had shattered my self-confidence. I became quite negative and rebellious. However, the support of family, friends, and mentor helped me regain my self-confidence. Their belief in me, encouragement, and advice helped me get a fighting spirit and I started my perseverance to succeed with patience and positivity. Soon, acknowledgments, successes, rewards, recognition boosted my self-confidence. An American friend told me not to hesitate to speak English as at least, I know two languages while she knows only one. This was a realization.

Learning: Self-confidence results in unveiling one's true potential

Self-confidence is critical for knowing and realizing true potential. Self-confidence can be built at any stage of life by following principles of positivity, self-belief, self-affirmation, perseverance, passion, ignoring toxic people, doing things you like, and stop comparing with others.

The Courage: It is never too late to do anything

My biggest learning on 'Courage' came from the experience of John, a person in his 50s, in the Sears project. I remember him struggling for work, and restless in his chair, but he did not hesitate in asking my help. He highly appreciated my help. When I asked him, as to what he was doing earlier, he said 'Painting'. I could not understand and thought it may be on specialized software for the painting field.

"I have been painting houses for over 25 years and was getting $20-$25 per hour rate for it, while I see young IT guys coming and getting $150-$200 per hour, then I decided, what the heck, I will also get into IT field. I did six months course and here I am," he clarified. I was shocked. A person inside me stood up and gave a big salute to John. Here is a 50+ guy who has been doing a painting job, which has nothing in common with software programming in IT, but he decided to learn and move into IT and had the guts and courage to do it.

"It's never late to do anything if one has the courage and resolve."

Lack of courage is like loss of opportunity. Courage also instils self-confidence. It is our mental block that stops us to be courageous.

Learning: Never too late to do anything; Courage-Initiative helps

It is never too late to do what you want to do. Courage helps increase confidence and take initiative. Courage helps explore new options and opportunities. Courage either results into success or at least learning.

The Formula = Take Initiative, Identify Problem, Create Solution.

(Initiative + Curiosity) + (Creativity + Innovation) = Learning + Growth

Being curious and taking initiative is a very important trait of one's behavior. My habit of taking initiatives with curiosity has led to identifying needs/problems/issues. Creativity and innovation then result in a good solution. Together this results in huge learning, achievement, growth, and satisfaction. It has helped me learn more, get recognized, and placed me in a league of 'Thinker' and 'Performer' most of the time in an organization. Some of the initiatives that I took:

Initiative in Technical Education department, helped me create an automation system resulting in huge benefits. Gave me huge learning, confidence, recognition, and satisfaction. Grew my stature.

Curious look at the redundancy in desperate systems led me to take initiative to develop an ERP application for Raymond. This gave me huge learning, satisfaction, and growth besides building ERP career.

Initiative to develop PeopleSoft practice in Rapidigm gave huge learning and exposures of sales, presales, hiring, and COE. This helped me immensely during that time and also later in my career.

Learning: Initiatives enhance knowledge; Places you high in position.

An organization has more followers than thinkers. Proactive initiatives to identify problems and solving them, over and above assigned tasks is considered 'Exceeding Performance' and accordingly rewarded. This uplifted my positioning as a leader, thinker and a go-getter in the organizations. Tools like Six Sigma and Kaizen help immensely in this.

Excellence with fun: Ensures the sustainable and enjoyable journey

World over, people are facing challenges of 'Work-Life Balance' and are struggling to find a balance between work time and personal time.

We spend half of our active time working on an office job (Work Time). If the job is according to our passion, then it keeps us rejuvenated but if it is not then we get a feeling of fatigue after a time. Work can be made interesting through quality of work, learning, aligning to passion, creativity, initiative and innovation. Additionally, the work atmosphere also makes a huge impact in work excellence. On the other hand, the fun part can be divided into two parts – fun at work space and fun in personal life. Fun at work space is related to work atmosphere and depends on hygiene and people. Fun in personal space depends on quality time spent in one's personal life. I observed that PK had created a good work atmosphere in the office which helped us. Later, in the World Bank project, the work part was not to my satisfaction so, I had to take new initiatives to make it interesting but the atmosphere there was not fun at all. As a result, despite success at work, I got bored soon. At Raymond Consultancy, work was challenging with fantastic learning besides the fun atmosphere was quite good. It kept me rejuvenated and creative.

Learnings: Excellence with Fun is critical; Ensures enjoyable work-life

Balance of good work and an environment of fun is critical for success. This results in unleashing the power in self while staying rejuvenated.

The Magnificent P's: My Experiential Life Mantra for success

During this phase of my life, I evolved a formula that helps in success. **"Purposeful Perseverance with Patience, Passion, Positivity and Play realizes the Power of self, achieve Pride, and ultimately Progress in life"**. The P's played a huge role in my life and for those around me.

Purpose: It is important to have purpose in terms of tasks, targets, destination or dream without which no action can have a direction.

Perseverance: Whatever is the purpose, it does not get served on a platter. One has to persevere to fulfil the purpose.

Patience: In the journey of perseverance, there may be difficulties and having patience is important to continue the perseverance.

Passion: Passion gives intense enthusiasm towards purpose. It creates interest, enthusiasm, excitement for the purpose and instils energy.

Positivity: Positivity is much-needed during perseverance, to help face challenges. One needs the "half-glass filled approach.

Play: Play is the fun element to remain rejuvenated.

Power: By working on above P's one can realize the Power of self.

Pride: It is important to believe and take pride in what you do.

Progress: Fine-tuning these P's as per the need can realize Progress.

Learning: The magnificent 'Ps' can be used as levers that need to be fine-tuned according to the need of a person to achieve success.

The Power of Self: Yog Nidra as discovered on the curves of my life

One of the critical learning I got from my mentor PK was about Yog Nidra while working in 24X7 mode.

Yog Nidra is a form of guided meditation also known as "yogic sleep" or "effortless relaxation." There is evidence that Yog Nidra helps relieve stress. The purpose of introducing Yog Nidra to me was to get much-needed relaxation quickly, so that I can continue my hard work.

There is a recorded technique comprising of certain steps to be initially performed under the guidance of an expert. PK did play that role for me. After my first session of about 40 minutes, I felt like I have slept for hours and my body and soul felt very relaxed and rejuvenated. I was amazed at this learning and since, I desperately wanted to learn and grow faster, I started working in crazy 24X7 mode and practiced Yog Nidra to get much-needed relaxation and rejuvenation in a short time. However, I soon realized that this technique is powerful and hence must be practiced with restraint.

Learning: Yog Nidra is a powerful technique; One needs to be careful

Yog Nidra is a very powerful tool for relaxation and reducing stress. In busy work life, working long hours and in stressful environment often leads to lack of sleep and fatigue. Without being rejuvenated one's performance gets affected along with health. It needs to be practiced with great care and caution, so that it shall not get wrongly leveraged.

The Obstruction: "Kuchh toh log kahenge, Logo ka kaam hai kehna"

Rajesh Khanna sang "Kuchh to log kahenge, logo ka kaam hai kehna." Movie was *Amar Prem*, playback singer was Kishore Kumar. Lyricist, Anand Bakshi, touched the taboo of society "People will say something or the other, it's their business to talk, ignore it, lest…".

I have seen people around me who have been the victim of this syndrome of 'what will people say?' This is because of the habit of "intrusion into other person's matters" by the people and passing critical judgment. This hampers people in many ways:

- Over consciousness, leading to inaction, or wrong action at times
- Not asking a genuine question in a class, meeting, interaction.
- Not following one's dream due to the fear of rejection by other.
- Worry of taking risks and failures – hampers many possibilities
- I faced this in initial part of my life:
- Rebel and Retaliation part of my life was due to society comments.
- Not completed M.Sc. thinking what will people say.
- Hesitating to submit my first assignment in Sears.

Learning: Move on from "What will people say?" to "Let them say…"

Different people, different thoughts. People will pass judgement. Do not miss anything based on what others say. Focus on your passion, thoughts and take action without worries. Either you will succeed or learn by taking an action, there is nothing to lose.

The Perspective: Theory of Relativity – The Change is Constant

Theory of Relativity has two dimensions:

Dimension #1 (Others): Different people have different thinking, and understanding based on their knowledge, experience, environment, and interpretation. This is why what is right for one may not be right for others; what is unknown to one, may be known to others; what is ideal for one, may not be for others. It is very difficult to say what is right and what is wrong in general, unless, it is specified in the form of a law. I concluded that unless clearly defined in a context, it is wrong to pass judgment or impose one's thought on others. The best approach is to listen to understand others' perspectives and discuss the same to conclude if one 'Agrees to Agree' or 'Agrees to Disagree'. Hence, I realized that **'The Art of Listening'** is the most important trait.

Dimension #2 (Self): The knowledge, understanding, perspective, thinking, and belief changes with time. Time is constantly changing. My knowledge and understanding changed too as I got exposure over time. What I did not know earlier, I knew now; what was right earlier, is not now. The **change is constant** based on experience. I concluded that one has **to be open to keep on looking to adopt life changes** and not remain rigid on what was thought and decided earlier. Some people adopt this as '**Go with the Flow**' but, I think instead one should **'Keep Deliberating, Adopt Changes and take Appropriate Actions.'** based on the current situation, knowledge, and experience.

www.ingramcontent.com/pod-product-compliance
Ingram Content Group UK Ltd.
Pitfield, Milton Keynes, MK11 3LW, UK
UKHW040005200726
13854UKWH00001B/50

9 798885 214827